BITE SIZE

BITE SIZE

Elegant Recipes for Entertaining

FRANÇOIS PAYARD

with Anne E. McBride and Craig Freeman

PHOTOGRAPHS BY ROGÉRIO VOLTAN

WM

WILLIAM MORROW

An Imprint of HarperCollinsPublishers

For Alexandra

The life of a chef is harsh. Our work requires us to be in the kitchen when most people are relaxing and socializing, and we often forget to say thank you to the people closest to us.

For the past thirteen years, while I have been in the kitchen and at the forefront of Payard, my wife, Alexandra, has encouraged my dreams and shared my vision. Her unfailing support and warmth help me and our business every day. With Tastings, our catering company, she has charmed customers with her efficiency and her conviviality. Tastings would not be as successful as it is without her. This is my opportunity to thank Alexandra and to tell her how much her support means to me.

I hope that what you see in the following pages will inspire you to go into your kitchen and invite your friends. It would be a shame not to share tastes like these, as they were created out of love.

❖

HarperCollins books may be purchased for educational, business, or sales promotional use. For information please write: Special Markets Department, HarperCollins Publishers, 10 East 53rd Street, New York, NY 10022.

FIRST EDITION

Designed by Vertigo Design NYC

Printed on acid-free paper

LIBRARY OF CONGRESS CATALOGING-IN-PUBLICATION DATA

Bite size : elegant recipes for entertaining / François Payard
    p. cm.
ISBN-13: 978-0-06-088722-3
ISBN-10: 0-06-088722-2
  1. Appetizers. 2. Entertaining. I. Title.

TX740.P375 2006
641.8 12—dc22   2006041230

06 07 08 09 10 ❖/TP 10 9 8 7 6 5 4 3 2 1

CONTENTS

ACKNOWLEDGMENTS

To chef Philippe Bertineau, my colleague, confidant, and friend, for seeing that the quality of every Tastings event is comparable to the restaurant's high standards. Payard would not be the same without him. To Craig Freeman, the chef of my downtown restaurant InTent, who remains calm, respectful, responsible, and professional even during the most stress-filled times. To Adilson Soares, for introducing Brazilian-inspired canapé ideas and developing a new line of decorative serving trays. And after working for three years as Payard's sous-chef, Ken Tajima is now the catering chef, infusing Japanese culture into his culinary wonders.

To Romain Arnaud, who is always working behind the scenes, overseeing all waiters in Napoleonic fashion and orchestrating all Tastings events. And to Nicolas Néant and Cyrille Chaminade, the two pastry chefs who have been absolutely indispensable in preparing all of Payard's confectionaries.

To photographer Rogério Voltan, a long-time friend and collaborator, for so beautifully portraying the Payard passion through the graceful angle of his lens.

To Anne E. McBride, terrific friend and writer, so precise and detail-oriented and such a gem to work with.

Once again, to Harriet Bell at William Morrow, for her confidence in my work and for the collaboration she makes of publishing a book.

To all the cooks, pastry chefs, and staff members whose talent and dedication are an indispensable part of our team.

To my family, for its support and education, which have been fundamental in my life and career.

And, of course, very special thanks to all of Payard's clients and guests for being such a wonderfully dedicated part of our family. Where would we be without you?

FROM MY PARTIES TO YOURS

In 2002, five years after I opened Payard, my pâtisserie and bistro in New York City, my wife, Alexandra, added a catering branch to our business: Tastings by Payard. We started with a few small parties here and there, and now we cater several events a week for hundreds of people. At these cocktail parties guests eat finger foods—hors d'oeuvres, or small bites, as we call them—while standing up and sipping champagne or other drinks. Often they make a meal of the small bites, and sometimes they even sit down around a table to enjoy them. We call such evenings *dînatoires*.

A successful bite-size dish allows you to taste the various components—contrasting textures and flavors—while eating just one morsel. *Bite Size* is a collection of my favorite recipes. They have all been adapted for the home kitchen so that you can easily replicate them with readily available equipment and ingredients. I have included a few more elaborate recipes, as well, to keep you challenged. Each recipe makes about twenty servings and can easily be multiplied.

Organization is the secret to a successful party centered on small bites. Establish your menu in advance and make a plan of action for the couple of weeks before your party so that you have time to shop for everything and prepare a few items ahead of time. Mix and match dishes that can be prepared ahead with others that need to be assembled at the last minute, and serve a balance of hot and cold hors d'oeuvres.

When creating your menu, consider the number of guests you are expecting, how much time you have to prepare everything, how many dishes you want to offer, and, most important, what ingredients are in season. For an August party, prepare Cherry Tomatoes Filled with Goat Cheese (page 54), for example. Morel Ragoût in Gorgonzola Cream (page 69) is perfect for the spring, when fresh morels abound. Offer at least one vegetarian option. You can also pick a theme, such as a Mediterranean cocktail party.

If the party is a pre-dinner cocktail party, six to eight bites per person is enough; but if it is scheduled between 7 and 9 p.m., guests will usually eat ten to fifteen hors d'oeuvres in lieu of dinner. Try to serve one or two small bites at a time, rather than bringing them out all at once, so guests eagerly look forward to the next sampling.

Presentation is important also. Each individual bite should make an impression. We use Chinese soupspoons, edible vessels such as phyllo cups and endive leaves, shot or cordial glasses, cones, trays filled with spices or beans, flowers, glass trays, and so on.

When you entertain, the most important thing to remember is to enjoy yourself. The food is only one aspect of the evening. Fortunately, with these recipes, it's one aspect that is guaranteed to be a success.

EQUIPMENT

While you don't need a lot of fancy equipment to make the small bites in this book, the following items will make preparation easier. See the Resources section (page 167) for purchasing information.

ASSORTED ROUND COOKIE CUTTERS: You can buy round cutters separately, or pick up a box with sizes ranging from ½ inch to 4 or more inches in diameter for $16 to $20. Use them to cut toasts, puff pastry, and gelée into attractive servings. You'll find them in baking supply stores and online.

BAKING SHEETS: You should have at least two large baking sheets (about 12 × 18 inches) and one small one (about 15 × 11 inches). Use them for baking, parbaking, cooking meat, placing bites in the freezer, reserving food before assembling, and so on. Purchase them in the kitchenware section of any supermarket and at specialty stores.

CHINESE SOUPSPOONS: These are ideal for serving mouthfuls of otherwise hard-to-eat hors d'oeuvres. Buy either porcelain spoons or inexpensive plastic ones at Asian markets or online.

DEEP-FRYING THERMOMETER: Frying requires that the oil be at a precise heat, so invest in a thermometer that clips onto the side of a pot.

FINE-MESH SIEVE: Texture is really important when preparing bite-size dishes. By passing soups and other thick liquids through a fine-mesh sieve, you'll obtain a much smoother texture. Kitchenware stores carry them.

FLEXIPAN MOLDS: These nonstick, flexible pans are extremely practical and durable. They require no greasing, go in both the freezer and the oven, and unmold very easily. Find them in kitchenware stores or online.

MELON BALLER: These are available in kitchenware stores and supermarkets. Most have a small scoop and a larger one. They are useful for making perfect portion sizes and for hollowing out foods such as radishes and artichokes.

MICROPLANE GRATER/ZESTER: Nothing works like a Microplane for grating citrus zest. This high-end stainless steel grater/zester is also perfect for extracting the most flavor out of ginger. It will cost you about $10 in kitchenware stores or online.

MINI-MUFFIN PANS: These are used to make Tart Shells (page 10), Phyllo Cups (page 8), and other round bites. You should have at least two 12-cup pans or one 24-cup pan. The nonstick ones are ideal, but you can also use aluminum pans—just grease them well.

PLASTIC PASTRY BAGS OR RESEALABLE PLASTIC BAGS: Some small bites, such as those with fillings that go into cones or phyllo cups, are best shaped by piping them. You can use either type of bag for this, and you don't need any special tips—just a pair of scissors to cut an opening in the bag.

PARCHMENT PAPER: From lining baking sheets to making cone molds, parchment paper is essential when cooking and baking. Buy the unbleached kind at your supermarket.

PEPPERMILL FOR WHITE PEPPER: Almost all the recipes in *Bite Size* use freshly ground white pepper, for the round flavor it gives food. I also use white instead of black pepper to avoid noticeable black specks in the small bites. Kitchenware stores carry peppermills in many sizes and materials.

SILPAT: Silpats are nonstick washable silicone/fiberglass baking mats that can be used again and again and are ideal for many of the recipes in this book. These flexible mats, which come in many sizes, are placed on a baking sheet. They cost about $20 each, and you should have two. You'll find them in most kitchenware stores, in specialty stores, and online.

WIRE RACKS: Use wire racks to cool tuiles, crackers, and cones. Also place a rack over dough when baking it to keep it from puffing up, and over chorizo slices to keep them flat. You can find racks at your supermarket and in kitchenware stores.

SPECIALTY INGREDIENTS

Here are some unusual or hard-to-find ingredients that appear in the recipes. Other specialty ingredients, such as harissa and ponzu, which are only used once, are explained in those individual recipes.

FICELLE: A ficelle is a thin baguette, 10 inches long and 1½ inches wide. It is perfect for bite-size dishes because of its small size, but use a regular baguette if you can't find a ficelle.

FLEUR DE SEL: This "flower of salt" is one of the finest types of sea salt available; it is harvested by hand in France from the layer of salt that rises to the top of salt beds when the seawater evaporates. Because of its refined taste and distinct texture, it is mainly sprinkled on foods just before serving rather than used during the cooking process itself.

FOIE GRAS: Foie gras is available in grades A, B, and C. Grade A foie gras is the best available, with the fewest veins. It is the firmest kind and works best for cooking. Grade B has more veins and is softer, making it perfect for terrines. Avoid grade C, which is full of veins.

PANKO: These Japanese breadcrumbs are perfect for frying because they don't absorb as much oil as regular breadcrumbs do. As a result, fried foods remain crisp instead of turning soggy.

PASTRY FLOUR: This flour has a lower protein content than all-purpose flour and produces a finer crumb. While you can substitute cake flour, it is best to make your own pastry flour if you can't find it readily available. To make 1 cup of pastry flour, combine ¾ cup all-purpose flour with ¼ cup cake flour.

ROCK SALT: Rock salt is a very coarse type of salt. Because it is very chunky, it makes a great bed for foods such as oysters, and when combined with crushed ice on a tray, it keeps the ice from melting too fast.

TRUFFLE JUICE: Truffles are soaked in a brine and then pressed to extract the flavored liquid. Truffle juice is usually sold in small cans.

TRUFFLE OIL: Truffle oil, made by soaking white or black truffles in high-quality olive oil, has a very distinct earthy aroma. It is a great way to add truffle flavor to a dish at a rather reasonable cost.

THE BASICS

These basic recipes and techniques are used throughout *Bite Size*. They will make a real difference in the way you cook when entertaining because they'll allow you to work faster and in a more organized way, leaving you more time to enjoy yourself and your guests.

You can also incorporate these recipes and techniques into your daily cooking by making full-size tarts with the doughs, filling the phyllo cups with a variety of mousses, and baking loaves of bread with the burger bun recipe.

PEELING AND SEEDING TOMATOES

Any type of tomato—including plum, beefsteak, yellow, and even the small cherry and grape varieties—can be peeled by quickly blanching them in simmering water. The riper the tomato, the less time it will need in the water. Blanch the tomato just long enough to be able to easily peel away its skin but not actually cook the flesh. Use this technique when preparing White Anchovy and Tomato Crostini (page 124), Foie Gras Mousse with Tomato-Strawberry Jam (page 141), and Ratatouille in Parmesan Cups (page 65), for example. ❋ Place a pot of water on the stove over high heat and bring to a rapid boil. Fill a bowl with very cold water and ice cubes to make an ice water bath. With a small knife, remove the core of the tomato and slice a small "X" on the opposite end. Using a slotted spoon, slide the tomato into the boiling water and leave it there for 10 seconds. Then immediately plunge the tomato into the ice water bath to cool. Once the tomato is cool, peel the skin away.

PEELING BELL PEPPERS

The skin of bell peppers can be tough, which is particularly undesirable in a small bite. Unless a recipe specifically calls for roasting and peeling them, simply peel off the outer skin of bell peppers with a vegetable peeler before chopping them.

SEGMENTING CITRUS FRUITS

Segmenting citrus fruits, such as grapefruits, lemons, limes, or oranges, removes the bitter pith and the membrane. This technique is used for Lime Salmon on Potato Crisps (page 82), Scallop Ceviche with Grapefruit Gelée (page 74), and Kataifi-Wrapped Scallops with Orange-Mustard Sauce (page 121). ❋ Cut off a small slice from the top and bottom of the citrus fruit, and stand the fruit on one end. Slice down from the top of the fruit, cutting away the rind and the pith, following the curve of the fruit. Continue, making sure to remove all of the white pith as well as the rind. Then, holding the fruit in one hand, slice alongside the connective membrane on each side of each segment to easily release them.

CLARIFYING BUTTER

Clarified butter has a higher smoking point than regular butter, which means that it doesn't burn as quickly. It keeps indefinitely when covered and refrigerated. Use it to brush phyllo dough, or in dishes such as Croques Salmon (page 105), Seared Tuna with Tomato Confit (page 113), and Caesar Salad Spring Rolls (page 31). Two cups (4 sticks) of unsalted butter will yield 1½ cups of clarified butter. ❋ Melt the butter in a deep pot over medium-high heat and bring it to a simmer. Using a spoon, skim off the foam that rises to the top. Turn the heat to low and simmer for about 10 minutes, or until all the milk solids fall to the bottom of the pot and the butter becomes clear. Strain the butter through a fine-mesh sieve lined with damp cheesecloth, leaving the milk solids behind. Cover and refrigerate.

TOASTING NUTS

Toasting nuts brings out their full flavor and gives them a more pronounced taste. Do this for the nuts used in Lamb Tenderloin with Endive, Roquefort, and Walnuts (page 145) and Crispy Polenta with Pesto and Parmesan (page 47), for example. ❋ Spread the nuts in a single layer on a baking sheet, and bake them in a preheated 325° F oven for 10 to 12 minutes, depending on the nuts. Shake the pan a couple of times during the process, and watch the nuts carefully so they don't burn. Remove the nuts from the oven as soon as you start to smell them.

SHUCKING OYSTERS

To shuck oysters for Kumamoto Oysters with Yuzu Sorbet and Caviar (page 85) or Leek and Oyster Tartlets (page 110), hold the oyster firmly in one hand, using a kitchen towel or an oyster glove (such as the silicone ones sold at Williams-Sonoma) for protection. Place the tip of an oyster knife in the hinge between the top and bottom shells, and run it along the length of the shell. Then twist the knife to open the shell, and cut the tough muscle that connects the oyster to the shell.

RICE PAPER

Rolls such as Duck Spring Rolls with Pickled Vegetables (page 131) and Vegetable Spring Rolls with Guacamole (page 29) are made with rice paper, a very thin, edible paper made from rice flour and water. It comes in square or round sheets that are almost translucent and very brittle. The technique takes a little bit of practice to master, so, at first, have a few extra pieces on hand. Place about $1/4$ cup of very hot but not boiling water in a bowl and soak the rice paper in it one sheet at a time until it becomes soft and pliable. Keep an eye on the paper while it is soaking so that you can remove it at just the right moment. This will take between 30 seconds and 1 minute. If the paper is too dry, it will break, and if it is too wet, it will tear. Remove the paper from the water, pat it dry with a kitchen towel, and place it on a damp towel to prepare your roll. Once you get the hang of it, which won't be long, you'll enjoy making a wide range of spring rolls.

PARCHMENT PAPER CONE MOLDS

You can buy cone-shaped molds in baking supply stores or online (see Resources), or you can make your own out of parchment paper. Use these molds to make Tuna Tartare in Sesame Cones (page 89), Salmon Rillettes Cones (page 93), and Smoked Trout Rillettes Cones (page 95). ❋ Cut out ten 8 × 12-inch pieces of parchment paper. Cut each rectangle in half diagonally, forming two right triangles. Hold a triangle by the middle of its long side between the thumb and forefinger of your left hand. The top edge should be lined up straight. Grab the left corner between your right thumb and forefinger and roll it to the top right corner, forming a cone shape. Hold the two corners together with your right hand, and fold the bottom side around, bringing its corner to the other two and completing the cone shape. Fold all three corners into the cone to keep it closed. Repeat with the remaining paper, to form 20 cones.

Phyllo Cups

MAKES 24

PHYLLO CUPS ARE BEST with solid fillings—liquids will seep through—such as Pea Purée and Ricotta Salata (page 61). You need one 24-cup mini-muffin pan or two 12-cup ones. Stored in an airtight container, the phyllo cups will keep for up to a week.

5 sheets phyllo dough, thawed if frozen
½ cup melted clarified butter (page 6)

1. Preheat the oven to 400° F.

2. Place 1 sheet of phyllo on a work surface and brush it with clarified butter. (Keep the remaining phyllo covered with a towel to prevent it from drying out.) Place another sheet of phyllo on top of the first sheet, and brush it with clarified butter. Repeat the process with the remaining sheets of phyllo. Do not butter the top sheet.

3. Once all the sheets are stacked and buttered, cut out 20 rounds of phyllo with a 2-inch cookie cutter. Place the rounds in the cups of a Flexipan mold or a mini-muffin pan, and bake for 10 minutes or until golden brown.

4. Remove from the oven and let cool slightly. Then unmold by gently twisting the cups out of the molds. (They will not stick because of the butter used, but they will be fragile.) Store in an airtight container at room temperature for up to 1 week.

Yeast Dough

MAKES ENOUGH FOR AT LEAST 24 ROUNDS

YOU CAN FREEZE THIS extremely versatile dough uncooked, whole or cut into rounds, tightly wrapped, for up to two months. It will also keep in the refrigerator for up to three days. Use it to make Scallop and Black Truffle Pizzas (page 109), a full-size Tarte Flambée (page 163), or any other type of savory tart.

1¼ teaspoons active dry yeast
⅓ cup warm (110° to 115° F) water
2 cups all-purpose flour
¾ teaspoon salt
1 large egg, beaten
4 teaspoons olive oil

1. Sprinkle the yeast over the water in a small bowl, and let it stand for 10 minutes, until the yeast begins to foam.

2. Place the flour and salt in a large bowl and make a well in the center. Pour the yeast mixture, egg, and olive oil into the well. Starting in the middle of the well, gradually stir the flour into the liquid, making even larger circles with a fork or a whisk. Continue until the dough comes together. Then knead the dough for a few seconds to make a ball. Cover the dough with a damp towel and let it rise in the refrigerator for 4 hours.

3. If you are making parbaked dough rounds, skip to the recipe below. Otherwise, remove the dough from the refrigerator and punch it down. If using it immediately, roll it out on a lightly floured surface and use it as directed in the recipe. Or wrap the ball of dough tightly in plastic wrap and freeze it for up to 2 months.

Parbaked Dough Rounds

1. Preheat the oven to 450° F.

2. Remove the risen dough from the refrigerator and punch it down. Dust a work surface lightly with flour, and roll the dough out in all directions until it is 1/16 inch thick. Place the dough on a baking sheet and bake for 3 minutes. (This step is essential for the dough to retain its shape—the dough should not be cooked but dry enough to pick up.)

3. Remove the baking sheet from the oven and lower the temperature to 400° F. Cut the dough into 1½-inch rounds with a cookie cutter. Place the rounds on an upside-down baking sheet, and cover them with another baking sheet, right side up. Bake for 6 to 8 more minutes, until crispy and light brown.

4. Remove from the oven and transfer the parbaked rounds to a plate to cool. Once cooled, the rounds can be stored in an airtight container for a day or two.

Tart Shells

THIS DOUGH IS CALLED a *pâte brisée* and can also be used for full-size tarts of all kinds. Cover it with foil before blind baking it so that it doesn't puff up. Vary the shape of these tarts by using square mini-muffin pans or various petit four molds, such as round or barquette shapes (see below). Bake them ahead of time and stack them on top of one another, wrapped in plastic wrap. Store them in an airtight container for two weeks, or freeze them for up to six months. Freeze any unused dough, tightly wrapped in plastic wrap. Use the small tart shells for Leek and Oyster Tartlets (page 110) and Foie Gras Mousse with Tomato-Strawberry Jam (page 141).

2 cups plus 1 tablespoon pastry flour

8 tablespoons (1 stick) plus ½ tablespoon cold unsalted butter, diced

1 teaspoon salt

5 tablespoons very cold water

1. Place the flour and cold butter in the bowl of an electric mixer fitted with the paddle attachment, and mix on low speed until the mixture has the texture of coarse cornmeal. Do not overmix. With the machine running, add the salt and slowly drizzle in the water just until the dough forms a ball. Remove the dough from the mixer, wrap it in plastic wrap, and let it rest for at least 1 hour in the refrigerator, or 30 minutes at room temperature.

2. Preheat the oven to 375° F. Spray the cups of a 24-count mini-muffin pan or two 12-count mini-muffin pans. Cut out 24 parchment paper rounds that are slightly larger than the muffin cups.

3. Roll the dough out in all directions until it is ⅟₁₆ inch thick. Using a 1½-inch cookie cutter, cut out 24 rounds of dough. Place them in the cups and trim off any dough that is hanging over the top. Place the scraps in a piece of cheesecloth and use it to lightly press the dough in each of the cups. This will remove any air bubbles. Let the dough rest at room temperature for 30 minutes.

4. Place a parchment paper round over each tartlet and fill it with rice or lentils. Bake for 15 minutes, or until the pastry is golden brown. Remove the pans from the oven and remove the rice-filled parchment liners. Allow the tart shells to cool in the pan.

5. When they have cooled, remove the tart shells from the cups by gently twisting them. Store on a baking sheet or a tray.

VARIATION: To make small individual molds such as barquettes, arrange 20 molds close to one another on a baking sheet and lay the sheet of ⅟₁₆-inch-thick dough over all of them. Roll a rolling pin over the molds to trim the dough, and remove the scraps. Press an empty mold inside each filled one. Then put an empty baking sheet on top of the molds (this will keep the dough from puffing up). Bake at 375° F for 15 to 20 minutes or until golden brown. Remove the baking sheet from the oven, and remove the top baking sheet and the empty molds. Let the tart shells cool in their molds on the baking sheet. When they have cooled, remove the tart shells from the molds.

Vol-au-Vents

MAKES 20 TO 24

A VOL-AU-VENT is a puff pastry shell that can be used with either savory or sweet fillings. You will see a recipe for Lobster Vol-au-Vents with American Sauce (page 106), but a creamy mushroom ragoût or a chicken stew would be delicious as well. On the sweet side, try an apple-raisin or plum-almond filling. When buying puff pastry, look for brands made with all butter, such as Dufour.

2 frozen puff pastry sheets (14 ounces each), thawed in the refrigerator
2 large eggs, beaten

1. Preheat the oven to 400° F. Line a baking sheet with parchment paper, and cut another sheet of parchment to the same size.

2. On a lightly floured surface, roll the puff pastry out in all directions until it is ¼ inch thick. Cut out 40 rounds of dough with a 1½-inch fluted cookie cutter.

3. Cut the center out of 20 rounds with a 1-inch fluted cookie cutter, and discard the centers. You should now have 20 rounds and 20 rings. Place the whole rounds on the prepared baking sheet, and brush them with the beaten egg. Place a puff pastry ring over each round. Place the other sheet of parchment paper on top, and then set a wire rack on top of it to keep the dough from puffing up too much.

4. Bake for 20 minutes, or until golden brown. Remove the baking sheet from the oven and lift off the wire rack. Let the vol-au-vents cool on the baking sheet. Fill with the desired filling.

Black Bread Mini Burger Rolls

MAKES 20

THESE BUNS GO WITH the Pork Burgers with Pickled Red Onions (page 154) or any other burgers, or you can fill them with tuna or chicken salad. No rye or buckwheat flour is used to make this bread black—just all-purpose flour that is toasted until it darkens. Freeze any leftover uncooked dough for up to a month, or bake it in a loaf pan, then slice it to make more canapés or sandwiches.

¾ cup all-purpose flour
2½ teaspoons (1 envelope) active dry yeast
1½ cups warm (110° to 115° F) water
2¾ cups bread flour
2 teaspoons salt

1. Preheat the oven to 400° F.

2. Spread the all-purpose flour on a baking sheet and bake it in the oven for 40 to 45 minutes, until it has a dark color and a toasted flavor.

3. Sprinkle the yeast over ¼ cup of the warm water in a small bowl, and let it sit for 10 min-

utes, until the yeast starts to foam. In an electric mixer fitted with the dough hook, stir together the toasted all-purpose flour, the bread flour, the remaining 1¼ cups warm water, and the yeast mixture. Mix on low speed for about 3 minutes, just until the wet and dry ingredients are incorporated. Add the salt and beat on medium speed for 3 to 6 minutes, until a soft dough forms and pulls away from the edges of the bowl.

4. On a lightly floured surface, roll the dough out in all directions until it is ½ inch thick. Cut out 20 rounds with a 1-inch cookie cutter. Cover the cut rounds with a damp towel and let them stand for 30 minutes.

5. Preheat the oven to 400°F. Line a baking sheet with parchment paper.

6. Place the rolls on the prepared baking sheet and bake for 15 to 20 minutes, until they are brown and crusty. Remove from the oven and let them cool on the baking sheet.

VEGETABLES

Vegetable bites should be plentiful at any party, not only for vegetarian guests but because they are the best expression of the season, showcasing their ingredients at their peak. Feel free to adapt the recipes based on the vegetables you find at the market. Not all the recipes here will suit vegetarians, since some include meat or fish. For strict ovo-lacto vegetarians, you can use vegetable stock instead of chicken stock and soy milk instead of regular milk. In many instances, you can omit the cream, bearing in mind that the taste of the dish will be less rich.

Chilled Asparagus Soup

Too OFTEN, ASPARAGUS SOUP is an unappealing, murky gray-green. This version, however, conjures notions of spring, with its bright green color, achieved by puréeing the asparagus while still hot before immediately shocking them in the ice water. Cooling them down so rapidly preserves the chlorophyll in the vegetable. ❈ Make the soup a day ahead and store it in the refrigerator.

40 asparagus spears
¼ cup olive oil
½ cup sliced shallots
¾ cup sliced leeks, white part only, thoroughly rinsed
6 cups chicken stock
Fine sea salt
Freshly ground white pepper
¾ cup heavy cream
Grated zest of 1 lime

1. Place a large pot of water over high heat and bring to a boil. Fill a bowl with very cold water and ice cubes to make an ice water bath.

2. While the water is heating, clean the asparagus by removing any brown or woody parts from the stalks. Cut 2-inch lengths from the tips down, and reserve the tips separately.

3. Salt the boiling water and add the asparagus tips. Cook until they are tender-crisp, about 3 minutes. Remove them from the water with a slotted spoon, and immediately place them in the ice water bath to cool them down.

4. Heat the olive oil in a large pot over medium-high heat. Add the shallots and leeks and cook until soft, 4 to 5 minutes. Add the asparagus bottoms, cover, and cook for another 5 to 10 minutes. Add the chicken stock and bring to a simmer. Reduce the heat to medium-low and let the soup simmer for 30 minutes.

5. Prepare a second water bath in a bowl large enough to contain another one. Transfer the soup to a blender and purée until smooth. Season it with salt and pepper, and pass it through a fine-mesh sieve into a bowl. Immediately place the bowl into the ice water bath to rapidly cool down the soup. Stir in ¼ cup of the cream. You can refrigerate the soup if you want, but it should be cold enough from the ice water bath.

6. Using a hand-held whisk or an electric mixer, whisk the remaining ½ cup cream, the lime zest, and a pinch of salt in a bowl until soft peaks form.

7. Divide the soup among 20 shot glasses, filling them about two-thirds full. Garnish each glass with 2 asparagus tips and a small spoonful of the lime cream. Arrange on a platter, and serve cold.

Chilled Tomato Soup with Guacamole

THIS SOUP, SERVED IN SHOT or other small glasses, is a refreshing twist on the standard salsa/guacamole combination—and a convenient one too, since you can make the soup a day ahead. Serve it chilled but not icy cold, or the full flavor of the tomatoes won't come through.

FOR THE SOUP:

2 tablespoons extra virgin olive oil

½ medium Spanish onion, chopped

1 celery stalk, chopped

½ fennel bulb, chopped

1 red bell pepper, seeds and ribs removed, chopped

4 garlic cloves, chopped

1 bouquet garni (1 thyme sprig, 1 rosemary sprig, 2 parsley sprigs, and 3 basil sprigs, all tied together with kitchen twine)

8 large, very ripe beefsteak tomatoes, cut into 8 pieces each

Fine sea salt

Freshly ground white pepper

4 drops Tabasco sauce

¼ teaspoon celery salt

FOR THE GUACAMOLE:

½ ripe avocado, coarsely chopped

Grated zest and juice of ½ lime

1 tablespoon finely chopped red onion

½ jalapeño pepper, seeds and ribs removed, finely chopped

¼ red bell pepper, peeled, seeded and finely chopped

1 cilantro sprig, chopped

Fine sea salt

Freshly ground white pepper

FOR THE GARNISH:

20 basil leaves

1. Heat the olive oil in a stockpot over medium-high heat. Add the onion, celery, fennel, bell pepper, and garlic. Cook for 10 minutes, until very soft. Do not let the vegetables brown. Add the bouquet garni, tomatoes, and 2½ cups water. Bring to a boil and cook for 15 minutes, or until the tomatoes have softened. Season with salt and pepper.

2. While the soup is cooking, fill a large pot with very cold water and ice cubes to make an ice water bath. When the soup is ready, place the stockpot in the ice water bath to cool. Remove the bouquet garni.

3. When the soup has cooled, transfer it to a blender and purée until smooth. Pass the purée through a fine-mesh strainer into a bowl. Add the Tabasco sauce and celery salt, and season to taste with salt and pepper. Set the soup aside.

4. Place the avocado in a small bowl and mash it with a fork until smooth. Stir in the lime zest and juice, red onion, jalapeño, bell pepper, and cilantro, and season with salt and pepper.

5. Ladle the chilled soup into 20 small glasses or bowls. Place a spoonful of the guacamole in the center of each one, and garnish with a basil leaf. Arrange on a platter, and serve cold.

Cauliflower Panna Cotta with Salmon Roe

MAKES ENOUGH FOR 20 SMALL GLASSES

PANNA COTTA, AN EGGLESS custard, is most often served as a dessert, but the texture and color of cauliflower lend themselves to this creamy preparation. The salmon roe adds just the right amount of saltiness to punch up the taste of the cauliflower. Play with this dish by using yellow or green cauliflower varieties, which American caviar would colorfully complement.
✽ I serve the panna cotta in cordial glasses, but shot glasses or any other type of small glass will do too.

14 ounces (about ½ head) cauliflower
1 tablespoon unsalted butter
2 cups cold heavy cream
2 teaspoons (1 envelope) unflavored gelatin
Fine sea salt
Freshly ground white pepper
1 ounce salmon roe

1. Cut the cauliflower into small pieces and place them in a pot. Add the butter and just enough water to cover about one third of the cauliflower. Cover the pot and bring to a simmer over medium heat. Simmer until the cauliflower is very tender, about 6 minutes. Drain off any excess water, and purée the cauliflower in a food processor.

2. Place the cream in a small pot and sprinkle the gelatin over it. Let it sit for 4 to 5 minutes, then bring to a simmer over medium-low heat to dissolve the gelatin. Remove the pot from the heat and let the cream cool to room temperature. Then gently mix it into the cauliflower purée. Do not whip it. Pass the mixture through a fine-mesh sieve into a bowl, and season to taste with salt and pepper.

3. Place twenty 1½-ounce cordial glasses on a baking sheet or a tray (it makes them easier to transfer in and out of the refrigerator). Fill each glass with the panna cotta. Cover the top of the glasses with plastic wrap and refrigerate until completely chilled, about 1 hour. This can be done up to a day ahead.

4. Remove the shot glasses from the refrigerator a few minutes before serving. Garnish each glass with ¼ teaspoon salmon roe. Arrange the glasses on a platter, and serve while still cold.

Quail Eggs with Russian Salad

MAKES 20

S ALADE RUSSE, OR RUSSIAN SALAD, was created by the French cooks of the Russian tsars. It features various vegetables cut in even pieces and bound with mayonnaise. In this recipe the traditional preparation is given a twist by serving it in quail eggs. Because the salad has to fit into the tiny eggs, it is important that the vegetables be cut in cubes that are as small and even as possible. Alternatively, you can serve the salad in the hollowed-out halves of ten hard-cooked large chicken eggs, the way you fill deviled eggs. If you do so, double the amount of vegetables and mayonnaise.

20 quail eggs
½ cup finely diced carrot
½ cup finely diced celery
½ cup finely diced turnip
½ tablespoon chopped rinsed capers
1 tablespoon minced cornichons
¼ cup mayonnaise
Freshly ground white pepper
Chopped chives or micro greens

1. Place the quail eggs in a pot and cover with cold water. Bring to a boil over high heat and let the eggs cook for 5 minutes. Then drain the eggs and run them under cold water to cool.

2. Peel the eggs and cut off the top of each one with a small knife, leaving about three-fourths of the egg whole. Set the tops aside. Carefully remove the yolk by gently pinching it out, making sure not to rip or tear the egg white. Cut off a very small sliver from the bottom of the hollowed-out eggs so that they can sit flat, and set them aside.

3. In a small bowl, finely chop the egg yolks and tops.

4. In a medium bowl, mix the carrot, celery, turnip, capers, cornichons, mayonnaise, and the chopped eggs, and season with pepper.

5. Fill the hollowed-out eggs with the salad mixture, and garnish the tops with chives or micro greens. Arrange the eggs on a platter and serve.

Sesame "Tofu" with Sour Cherry Topping

MAKES 20

After receiving many requests for a tofu dish, we came up with this "tofu" made with sesame paste and milk instead of soybean curd. Sesame paste, also known as tahini, is found in supermarkets, either in the natural foods section or with the spreads and preserves. Keep it refrigerated, and stir it well before using, as the oil separates from the paste. ❀ While the crackers are easy to make, you can substitute store-bought rice or sesame crackers.

FOR THE CRACKERS:

1 cup all-purpose flour
2 tablespoons very cold unsalted butter, diced
½ teaspoon baking powder
Fine sea salt
¼ cup very cold water
2 teaspoons black sesame seeds
2 teaspoons white sesame seeds
1 large egg, lightly beaten

FOR THE TOFU:

⅔ cup plus 2 teaspoons cornstarch or arrowroot
3 cups whole milk
3 tablespoons cream cheese
¼ cup tahini
Pinch of salt
Pinch of freshly ground black pepper

FOR THE TOPPING:

½ cup red wine
2 tablespoons sugar
1 tablespoon lemon juice
12 fresh cherries, pitted

1. Place the flour and butter in the bowl of an electric mixer fitted with the paddle attachment. Beat on low speed until the mixture has the texture of coarse cornmeal. Add the baking powder, salt, and cold water, and continue mixing just until the dough forms a ball, 30 seconds to 1 minute. Mix in the black and white sesame seeds. Remove the dough from the mixer, wrap it in plastic wrap, and let it rest in the refrigerator for at least 1 hour.

2. Preheat the oven to 350° F. Line a baking sheet with parchment paper.

3. On a lightly floured surface, roll the dough out in all directions until it is ⅛ inch thick. Cut out rounds of dough with a 1-inch cookie cutter. Place the rounds on the prepared baking sheet and brush with the beaten egg. Place in the oven and bake for 15 minutes, or until golden brown. Remove from the oven and let cool on the baking sheet. (You will have more crackers than necessary for this dish, but you can freeze the leftovers, tightly wrapped, for up to 1 month.)

4. Line a flat, shallow (½-inch-deep) dish with plastic wrap.

5. Place the cornstarch and ½ cup of the milk in a bowl, and whisk to combine. Place the remaining 2½ cups milk, cream cheese, tahini, salt, and pepper in a small pot over medium-high heat. Bring to a boil, and add the cornstarch mixture. Lower the heat to medium and cook for 10 minutes, stirring often. Place the cooked mixture in the prepared dish and refrigerate until it is completely cooled, at least 45 minutes.

6. Place the wine, sugar, and lemon juice in a pot and bring to a boil over high heat. Then remove it from the heat and add the cherries. Refrigerate until cold, about 20 minutes. Then cut the cooled cherries into small cubes. You can make this a day ahead; keep the cherries in the liquid, covered and refrigerated.

7. Remove the "tofu" from the plastic wrap and cut it into rounds with the 1-inch cutter. Place a round of "tofu" on top of each sesame cracker, and top with the diced cherries. Arrange on a platter, and serve cold.

Vegetable Frittata

THIS FRITTATA REMINDS ME of the potato omelets my grandmother made every Sunday, but the vegetables here are layered in a loaf pan to make a frittata cake, which can then be easily sliced. It makes for a stunning presentation, especially if blue potatoes are incorporated. Because frittatas can be served warm or made a day ahead, refrigerated, and offered at room temperature, they are a versatile party dish.

1 tablespoon unsalted butter, softened

2 red bell peppers

Olive oil

1 blue or Idaho potato, cut into ⅛-inch-thick slices

1 large leek, white part only, thinly sliced and thoroughly rinsed

1 small eggplant, cut into ⅛-inch-thick slices

2 medium zucchini, cut into ⅛-inch-thick slices

3 large eggs

1 tablespoon chopped basil

1 tablespoon grated Parmesan

Fine sea salt

Freshly ground white pepper

1 cup scallion cream cheese (see Note)

16 niçoise olives, pitted and halved

1. Preheat the oven to 400° F. Spread the butter on the sides and bottom of an 8 × 4 ½-inch loaf pan.

2. Cut the bell peppers in half and remove the ribs and seeds. Coat the peppers with olive oil, place them on a baking sheet, and roast in the oven for 15 to 20 minutes, until the skin begins to wrinkle. Remove from the oven, leaving the oven on, place them in a bowl, and cover with plastic wrap to create steam. Leave covered for 15 minutes. Then remove the skin by gently rubbing the peppers. Slice thinly and set aside.

3. Bring a small pot of water to a boil over high heat. Salt the water, add the potato slices, and cook just until you can pierce them with a knife without resistance, about 6 minutes. Drain the potato slices and let them cool.

4. Place enough olive oil in a sauté pan to coat the bottom, and heat it over medium-high heat. Add the leek and cook until tender, 3 minutes. Remove the leek from the pan and reserve. Add oil to the pan if necessary, and cook the eggplant, and then the zucchini, on both sides until nicely browned, about 2 minutes per side.

5. Lightly beat the eggs in a bowl. Add the basil and Parmesan, and season with salt and pepper.

6. Line the bottom of the loaf pan with the potatoes, covering the entire surface. Season with salt and pepper. Pour just enough of the egg mixture over the potato slices to cover them.

Then add a layer of eggplant slices on top of the potato, and season with salt and pepper. Pour a small amount of the egg mixture over the eggplant, and then continue, making a layer each of the bell peppers, leek, and zucchini, adding the egg mixture between the layers. Pour the remaining egg mixture over the top. Bake for 30 minutes. Then remove the pan from the oven and let the frittata cool in the pan.

7. Once the frittata has cooled, carefully unmold it by loosening the edges with a knife and turning the pan upside down on a cutting board. Trim the edges so that you can have squares with clean edges. Use a serrated knife to cut the frittata into 1-inch-thick slices. Cut each slice into 4 squares of about 1 inch.

8. Place a small amount of the scallion cream cheese on top of each square, and top with an olive half. Arrange on a serving platter, and serve warm or at room temperature.

NOTE: To make scallion cream cheese, place 1 cup cream cheese in the bowl of an electric mixer fitted with the paddle attachment. Mix on low speed, adding a little milk to loosen it. Turn the mixer off and stir in ¼ cup finely chopped scallions. Or you can purchase scallion cream cheese in the deli section of your supermarket.

Vegetable Spring Rolls with Guacamole

MAKES 24

GINGER BRINGS OUT THE FLAVOR of the vegetables in this dish, and the guacamole adds a rich and creamy texture. All the gustatory sensations come in one bite. Use hot but not boiling water for the rice paper.

FOR THE SPRING ROLLS:

2 celery stalks, strings removed, cut into pieces 6 inches long and ⅛ inch thick

3 tablespoons olive oil

Two 1-inch pieces of ginger, peeled and thinly sliced lengthwise

2 garlic cloves, crushed

1 carrot, cut into pieces 6 inches long and ⅛ inch thick

1 zucchini, cut into pieces 6 inches long and ⅛ inch thick

¼ cup very hot water

4 rice paper sheets

½ fennel bulb, cut into pieces 6 inches long and ⅛ inch thick

4 medium romaine lettuce leaves

Fine sea salt

Freshly ground white pepper

FOR THE GUACAMOLE:

1 ripe avocado

1 teaspoon finely chopped red onion

1 teaspoon finely chopped peeled red bell pepper

1 teaspoon finely chopped jalapeño pepper

1 teaspoon chopped cilantro

1 teaspoon lime juice

Fine sea salt

Freshly ground white pepper

1. Place a large pot of water over high heat and bring to a boil. Fill a bowl with very cold water and ice cubes to make an ice water bath. Salt the boiling water and blanch the celery for 2 minutes. Then drain and immediately place the celery in the ice water bath to cool.

2. Heat half of the olive oil in a sauté pan over medium-high heat, and add half of the ginger and half of the garlic. Add the carrot and sauté until cooked but still crisp, about 4 minutes. Remove the carrot, ginger, and garlic to a plate. Add the rest of the olive oil, ginger, and garlic to the pan. Sauté the zucchini until cooked but still crisp, about 3 minutes. Remove the zucchini, ginger, and garlic to a plate.

3. Place the hot water in a bowl and soak 1 sheet of the rice paper in it until it becomes soft and pliable. Depending on the temperature of the water, this will take between 30 seconds and 1 minute. Pat the rice paper dry with a kitchen towel and lay it on a damp towel.

4. Place 1 romaine leaf close to one edge of the rice paper. Place one-fourth of the fennel, celery, carrot, and zucchini in a straight line over the lettuce. Using the towel as a guide, slowly roll the paper around the vegetables, making the roll as tight as possible. Set the roll on a baking sheet and cover it with a damp towel.

5. Repeat with the other 3 sheets of rice paper and the remaining vegetables. Be sure to keep the spring rolls covered with a damp towel to prevent them from drying out. Refrigerate, covered with the damp towel, until ready to serve.

6. Scrape the flesh of the avocado into a bowl and mash it with a fork until smooth. Mix in the onion, bell pepper, jalapeño, cilantro, and lime juice, and season with salt and pepper. Cover and set aside in the refrigerator. (Because avocado tends to turn brown, it is best to not prepare the guacamole in advance.)

7. Using a serrated knife, trim off the ends of the rolls, and slice each roll into 6 pieces. Spoon a small amount of the guacamole on top of each spring roll. Arrange on a platter, and serve at room temperature.

Caesar Salad Spring Rolls

MAKES ABOUT 20

THIS ROLL IS MY ONE-BITE version of the classic Caesar salad, complete with dressing and all wrapped up in rice paper. All the flavors you'd expect in Caesar salad—anchovy, Parmesan, bread, and lettuce—are present. ❀ Rice paper is fragile, so have a couple of extra pieces available in case one tears.

FOR THE CAESAR DRESSING:

¼ cup mayonnaise
1 teaspoon grated Parmesan
2 anchovy fillets, minced

FOR THE CROUTONS:

2 tablespoons clarified butter (see page 6)
One ¼-inch-thick slice of white bread, crust removed, cut into ¼-inch cubes

FOR THE SPRING ROLLS:

¼ cup very hot water
3 rice paper sheets
6 prosciutto slices
3 romaine lettuce leaves, cut into long ¼-inch-wide strips
1 cup baby arugula

1. Using a fork or a spoon, mix the mayonnaise with the Parmesan and the anchovies in a bowl until everything is well incorporated. Fill a plastic pastry bag or a resealable plastic bag with the dressing, and set it aside. You can pre-pare the dressing ahead of time and keep it refrigerated for up to 1 day.

2. Heat the clarified butter in a sauté pan over medium-high heat. Add the bread cubes and stir gently with a wooden spoon so that they are all coated in butter. Sauté until golden brown, about 3 minutes, stirring a couple of times to make sure that the cubes toast on all sides. Set the croutons aside.

3. Place the hot water in a bowl and soak 1 sheet of the rice paper in it until it becomes soft and pliable. Depending on the temperature of the water, this will take between 30 seconds and 1 minute. Pat the rice paper dry with a kitchen towel and lay it on a damp towel.

4. Place 2 slices of the prosciutto close to the edge of the rice paper. (If you place it too close to the middle, you will have too many layers of rice paper without filling in your finished roll.) Arrange one third of the romaine and arugula over the prosciutto, stopping slightly before the edges. Roll the rice paper tightly around the prosciutto, romaine, and arugula, as you would for a sushi or a jelly roll. Set the roll on a baking sheet and cover it with a damp towel.

5. Repeat with the other 2 sheets of rice paper and the remaining prosciutto and greens. Be sure to keep the spring rolls covered with a damp

towel to prevent them from drying out. You can do this a couple of hours ahead of time and keep them refrigerated, covered with a damp towel.

6. When you are ready to serve them, trim the ends of each roll. (You can discard them if they are not filled, or keep them for yourself!) Slice each roll into ¾-inch-wide pieces, to make 6 or 7 pieces. Set each spring roll on one of its cut ends. You can do this directly on your serving platter.

7. Cut off a ¼-inch opening in the tip or corner of the pastry bag, and pipe a small dollop of the Caesar dressing on top of each roll. Place 3 toasted croutons on top of the dressing. Serve cold or at room temperature.

Pissaladières

MAKES 20

PISSALADIÈRE IS A TRADITIONAL DISH in the South of France, where I was born and raised. Typically it is made as a large pizza-style tart, but I serve it in small bites. ❈ This pissaladière is easy to prepare ahead of time. Cut the puff pastry into rounds as directed, and freeze them in a single layer on a baking sheet for one hour; then wrap tightly and freeze for up to a month. The onion can be cooked a day ahead and stored, covered, in the refrigerator. Just remember to take the puff pastry rounds out of the freezer 30 minutes before starting your dish, and reheat the onion on the stove or in the microwave. Freeze any leftover dough as is, or precut into rounds.

1 sheet frozen puff pastry (14 ounces), thawed in the refrigerator
1 large egg, lightly beaten
Olive oil
1 large Spanish or white onion, very thinly sliced
10 anchovy fillets
1 tablespoon cracked black peppercorns
10 niçoise olives, cut in half lengthwise and pitted

1. Preheat the oven to 425° F. Line a baking sheet with parchment paper.

2. On a lightly floured surface, roll the puff pastry out once to remove the fold marks.

3. Cut out 20 (or more) rounds of dough with a 2½-inch cookie cutter. Place the rounds on the prepared baking sheet and brush with the beaten egg. Cover with another piece of parchment paper, and place an empty baking sheet on top (this will keep the dough from rising too much or unevenly). Place in the oven and bake for 20 minutes, or until golden brown. Remove from the oven, take off the top baking sheet, and leave the pastry rounds on the baking sheet.

4. Place enough olive oil in a large sauté pan to coat the bottom, and heat it over medium heat. Add the onion and sauté until brown and caramelized, 7 to 8 minutes. When the onion is very well cooked, remove from the heat and place in the bowl of a food processor. Add the anchovies and pulse until the anchovies are mixed with the onion.

5. To assemble, put a small amount of the onion mixture on top of each puff pastry round, covering the entire surface. Sprinkle a little of the cracked peppercorns over the onion. Place the olive halves on top of the onion. Arrange on a platter, and serve warm or at room temperature.

Parsnip and Mushroom Tarts

MAKES 20

PHILIPPE BERTINEAU HAS BEEN the executive chef of Payard since we opened, and this is one of his signature recipes. The parsnip and mushroom combination makes it a perfect winter dish. All the components can be made ahead of time, and the tarts can be assembled two to three hours before they are baked.

1 sheet frozen puff pastry (14 ounces), thawed in the refrigerator
Extra virgin olive oil
4 small parsnips, thinly sliced
1 tablespoon unsalted butter
Fine sea salt
Freshly ground white pepper
10 small white mushrooms, cleaned and stemmed
Porcini oil
1 cup micro greens or mesclun

1. Preheat the oven to 400° F. Line a baking sheet with parchment paper.

2. On a lightly floured surface, roll the puff pastry out in all directions until it is ¼ inch thick. Cut out 20 rounds of dough with a 2-inch cookie cutter. Place the rounds on the prepared baking sheet, and place a wire rack over them (this will keep the rounds even and prevent them from rising too high). Bake for 20 minutes or until light golden brown. Remove from the oven, take off the wire rack, and let the pastry rounds cool on the baking sheet.

3. Place enough olive oil in a sauté pan to coat the bottom, and heat it over medium heat. Add the parsnips and cook until very tender, about 5 minutes. Remove the parsnips from the pan and place them in the bowl of a food processor. Purée (while still hot) until smooth, adding the butter. Season with salt and pepper. Pass the purée through a fine-mesh sieve into a bowl. Let cool completely, and reserve. You can make it a day ahead and store it, covered, in the refrigerator.

4. Cut the mushrooms into ⅛-inch-thick slices. Place enough olive oil in a sauté pan to coat the bottom, and heat it over medium heat. Add the mushrooms and cook until they are lightly browned, about 1 minute. Remove them from the heat. You can cook the mushrooms 2 to 3 hours ahead and store them, covered, in the refrigerator.

5. Preheat the oven to 375° F.

6. Spread a ¼-inch-thick layer of parsnip purée over each puff pastry round. Arrange a few mushroom slices over the purée, and season with salt and pepper. Drizzle with porcini oil, and arrange on a baking sheet. Bake for 15 minutes. Then remove the tarts from the oven and top each one with a little mound of micro greens. Arrange on a platter, and serve warm.

Asparagus and Pancetta Bundles

MAKES 20

Pancetta adds flavor, saltiness, and texture to this small bite. You can use prosciutto instead, but the results will be saltier. Save the asparagus bottoms for Chilled Asparagus Soup (page 15). ❋ This simple, quick dish can be further enhanced by a drizzle of hollandaise sauce. I include a version here if you want to make it.

40 asparagus spears
20 very thin pancetta slices
Olive oil
Hollandaise Sauce (optional; recipe follows)

1. Place a large pot of water over high heat and bring to a boil. Fill a bowl with very cold water and ice cubes to make an ice water bath.

2. Clean the asparagus by removing any brown or woody parts from the stems. Cut 2½-inch lengths from the tips down. Set the top pieces aside and reserve the bottoms for another use.

3. Salt the boiling water and add the asparagus. Cook until they are tender-crisp, about 3 minutes. Remove them from the water with a slotted spoon, and immediately place them in the ice water bath to cool them down.

4. Take 2 asparagus spears and hold them tightly together. Wrap 1 slice of pancetta snugly around the asparagus to make a tight bundle. Repeat with the remaining asparagus and pancetta.

5. Place enough olive oil in a large sauté pan to coat the bottom, and heat it over medium-high heat. Place a few asparagus bundles in the pan, taking care to not crowd the pan so you can turn them. Sauté the bundles until the pancetta is crispy, about 45 seconds on each side. Set the cooked bundles aside and sauté the rest.

6. Arrange the bundles, standing up, on a serving platter, with some hollandaise in a bowl if using. Serve warm.

SEE THE PHOTOGRAPH ON PAGE 13

Hollandaise Sauce

2 large egg yolks, beaten
1 cup clarified butter (see page 6), melted and warm
1 tablespoon lemon juice
Pinch of cayenne pepper
Fine sea salt

1. Fill a medium pot one-third full with water and bring it to a gentle simmer over medium heat. Place the egg yolks in a bowl that will fit snugly on top of the pot but not touch the water. Add 1 tablespoon cold water to the yolks. Reduce the heat to low and place the bowl over the pot. Cook slowly until the yolks start to thicken, 3 to 5 minutes, whisking constantly. Remove the bowl from the pot.

2. Slowly whisk the clarified butter into the yolks until all of the butter is incorporated. You want to emulsify the fat with the yolks, as if you were making mayonnaise. Whisk in the lemon juice and cayenne pepper, and season with salt. If the sauce is too thick, thin it down with a few drops of warm water.

3. Store the sauce in a warm place until ready to serve. (Ideally, make it after blanching the asparagus.) Serve it in a small bowl alongside the asparagus bundles.

Crispy Cauliflower Bites

MAKES 24

HERE, PLAIN CAULIFLOWER PURÉE is given a crispy new life by being frozen into little cakes and then fried. Freezing these bites makes them easier to roll in the breadcrumbs. It also means that they can be made in advance. Use one or two mini-muffin pans, or ¾-inch round molds if you have them.

½ cauliflower head
Olive oil
1 shallot, thinly sliced
2 tablespoons heavy cream
Fine sea salt
Freshly ground white pepper
1 quart canola oil, for frying
1 cup all-purpose flour
3 large eggs, lightly beaten
2 cups dried breadcrumbs

1. Line 20 mini-muffin cups with plastic wrap.

2. Cut the cauliflower into thin slices. Place enough olive oil in a large sauté pan to coat the bottom, and heat it over medium-high heat. Add the shallot and cook until translucent, about 5 minutes. Add the cauliflower, cream, and ¾ cup water and continue to cook until a knife easily pierces the cauliflower, about 10 minutes. Season with salt and pepper.

3. Purée the cauliflower mixture in a food processor, then pour it through a fine-mesh sieve into a bowl. Discard any of the cauliflower mixture left in the sieve. Fill a plastic pastry bag or a resealable plastic bag with the cauliflower purée, cut a ½-inch opening in the tip or corner, and pipe 2 teaspoons of the purée into each lined muffin cup. Place the muffin pan(s) in the freezer for about 1 hour, until the purée is frozen.

4. Fill a medium saucepan with the canola oil. Clip a deep-frying thermometer to the side of the pan, and heat the oil to 350° F.

5. Place the flour, eggs, and breadcrumbs in separate shallow containers. Remove the frozen purée from the molds by gently twisting them, and dip each one into the flour, then the eggs, and then the breadcrumbs.

6. Fry the breaded cauliflower bites, a few at a time, in the canola oil until golden brown, 5 to 7 minutes. Do not crowd the pan, and maintain the oil at a steady 350° F. As they are done, remove the cauliflower bites from the oil and place them on a plate lined with paper towels to drain. Sprinkle with salt.

7. Arrange on a platter, and serve warm.

NOTE: You can prepare these a couple of days ahead: Roll the frozen molds in the breadcrumbs. Place the breaded, frozen molds in heavy resealable plastic bags, and store in the freezer. Then proceed with frying just before serving.

Sweet Corn Madeleines with Caviar and Crème Fraîche

MAKES 20 TO 24

THESE SAVORY MADELEINES, similar to a light cornbread, are best when made with fresh corn. Roast the corn on an indoor or outdoor grill. Fresh cooked corn kernels or a small sprig of dill can be substituted for the caviar garnish.

Softened unsalted butter and all-purpose flour for the molds

2 ears fresh corn, roasted, kernels sliced off the cobs

1½ cups whole milk

2 large eggs

1 teaspoon sugar

½ cup fine yellow cornmeal

3 tablespoons all-purpose flour, sifted

1 teaspoon baking powder

Pinch of salt

1 tablespoon plus 1 teaspoon unsalted butter, melted

3 tablespoons very cold crème fraîche

1 ounce American caviar

1. Preheat the oven to 375° F. Brush a mini-madeleine mold with softened butter and dust it with flour.

2. In a blender, purée the roasted corn kernels with the milk.

3. In a mixer fitted with the paddle attachment, mix the eggs and sugar at low to medium speed until they become white and creamy, about 3 minutes. Add the cornmeal, puréed corn, flour, baking powder, and salt. Once the flour is incorporated into the batter, slowly mix in the melted butter.

4. Place the batter in a pastry bag or a resealable plastic bag, and cut a ¼-inch opening in the tip or corner. Pipe the batter into the prepared molds. Tap the molds lightly to remove any air bubbles from the batter and to prevent holes from forming in the madeleines.

5. Bake the madeleines for 8 to 10 minutes, or until lightly golden. Remove them from the oven, then unmold and arrange them on a platter.

6. Top each madeleine with a tiny dollop of crème fraîche and a few grains of caviar. Serve warm.

Panisse Fries with Anchovy Dipping Sauce

MAKES 20

PANISSE IS A CHICKPEA FRITTER from the South of France. Chickpea flour can be found in the natural foods section of supermarkets. Bob's Red Mill is a widely available brand. Store it in the freezer so that it doesn't turn rancid. For even more flavor, toast the flour before using it: cook it for a few minutes in a dry skillet over low heat, stirring with a wooden spoon so the flour doesn't burn.

FOR THE PANISSE:

1 quart chicken stock
2 tablespoons olive oil
Salt
Freshly ground white pepper
2½ cups chickpea flour

FOR THE DIPPING SAUCE:

3 anchovy fillets
1 teaspoon minced garlic
1 large egg yolk
1 cup olive oil
1 tablespoon lemon juice
Salt
Freshly ground white pepper

2 quarts canola oil, for frying

1. Line an 8-inch square cake pan with parchment paper. Place the chicken stock and olive oil in a small pot and season well with salt and pepper. Warm the liquid slightly over low heat; then whisk in the chickpea flour until the mix-ture is smooth. Turn the heat to high and whisk continuously until the flour is cooked and turns into a thick paste, 4 to 5 minutes. Remove the chickpea paste from the pot and spread it in an even ¼-inch-thick layer in the prepared pan. Refrigerate until the batter is completely cooled, at least 1 hour.

2. Place the anchovies and garlic in a small bowl. Mash them together with a fork, then mix in the egg yolk. Slowly whisk in the olive oil a little at a time, to create an emulsion as you would when making a vinaigrette. When the mixture be-comes thick, add the lemon juice. Then con-tinue to whisk in the remainder of the olive oil. (If the sauce becomes too thick, thin it with a little water.) Season with salt and pepper.

3. Fill a medium saucepan with the canola oil. Clip a deep-frying thermometer to the side of the pan, and heat the oil to 400° F.

4. Unmold the panisse over a cutting board, and cut it into 2-inch-long strips. Gently drop the strips into the oil in small batches, and fry until golden brown, about 2 minutes. Do not crowd the pan, and maintain the oil at a steady 400° F. As they are done, remove the strips from the oil and place them on a plate lined with paper tow-els to drain. Season with salt and pepper.

5. Stack the fries on a serving platter, or place them in a vertical vessel on the platter. Accompany with the anchovy sauce.

Crispy Polenta with Pesto and Parmesan

MAKES 20

POLENTA IS BETTER KNOWN for its texture than for its flavor, which is why it is such a good vehicle for other ingredients, like the pesto and Parmesan here.

FOR THE POLENTA:

2½ cups milk (regular, skim, or soy) or water
1 thyme sprig
1 rosemary sprig
1 garlic clove
Fine sea salt
Freshly ground white pepper
1 cup polenta or fine yellow cornmeal

FOR THE PESTO:

2 cups lightly packed basil leaves (about ½ bunch)
¼ cup pine nuts, toasted (see page 7)
1 tablespoon grated Parmesan
½ cup extra virgin olive oil
Fine sea salt
Freshly ground white pepper

Olive oil
4-ounce piece of Parmesan, shaved into pieces with a vegetable peeler

1. Line an 8-inch square cake pan with parchment paper, and cut another piece of parchment to the same size.

2. Place the milk, thyme, rosemary, and garlic in a pot over medium heat. Season with salt and pepper, and simmer for 5 minutes. Strain the milk into a bowl; discard the garlic and herbs. Return the milk to the pot and place it over low heat. Add the polenta in a slow stream while you whisk it in vigorously with the other hand. Cook for 20 minutes, stirring often, until smooth.

3. Pour the polenta into the prepared cake pan, and spread it out in an even ½-inch-thick layer. Cover with the other piece of parchment and refrigerate for about 1 hour. Cut the chilled polenta into 20 rounds with a 1-inch cookie cutter.

4. Bring a small pot of water to a boil over high heat. Fill a bowl with cold water and ice cubes to make an ice water bath. Blanch the basil leaves in the boiling water for 5 seconds. Remove them with a slotted spoon and immediately place them in the ice water bath to stop them from cooking further.

5. When the basil has cooled, drain it and pat dry. Place the basil, pine nuts, and grated Parmesan in a blender and purée. With the machine running, slowly drizzle in the olive oil through the top. Season with salt and pepper.

6. Place enough olive oil in a large sauté pan to coat the bottom, and heat it over medium-high heat. Sauté the polenta rounds until crispy and lightly browned on both sides, about 4 minutes a side. Remove them to a plate lined with paper towels to drain. Sprinkle with salt.

7. Top each polenta round with a dollop of pesto and a piece of shaved Parmesan. Arrange on a serving platter, and serve warm.

Prosciutto-Wrapped Gnocchi

MAKES 20

MAKE THE GNOCCHI dough as quickly as possible, while the potato is still hot, so it doesn't become gummy. Once shaped, the gnocchi can be frozen for up to a month.

1 large Idaho potato, scrubbed but not peeled
1 large egg yolk
½ cup all-purpose flour
Fine sea salt
Freshly ground white pepper
5 thin prosciutto slices, cut lengthwise into twenty ½-inch-wide strips
Olive oil

1. Preheat the oven to 400° F. Cut ten toothpicks in half.

2. Bake the potato for 1 hour, or until a knife can pierce through it without resistance. When the potato is cool enough to handle but still hot, peel it and pass it through a food mill set over a bowl.

3. Add the egg yolk, three-fourths of the flour, and salt and pepper to the potato, and gradually mix together with your hands. Work in the remaining flour a little at a time, adding only enough to give you a soft, light dough that does not stick to your hands. Adding too much flour will make the gnocchi heavy and tough.

4. Bring a large pot of water to a boil. Meanwhile, lightly flour a work surface and roll a golf-ball-size ball of dough into a long thin strip ½ inch in diameter. Cut the strip at ¾-inch intervals.

5. Place 1 piece of gnocchi on the tines of a fork and gently move it over the length of the tines with your thumb in a rolling motion, applying gentle pressure to leave a small indentation of your thumb on one side and an indentation of the fork on the other. Repeat with the remaining dough until you have 20 gnocchi.

6. Fill a bowl with very cold water and ice cubes to make an ice water bath. Salt the boiling water, and add the gnocchi. Cook the gnocchi for 2 to 3 minutes, or until they all rise to the surface. Remove the gnocchi from the pot with a slotted spoon, and immediately place them in the ice water bath to cool. When the gnocchi have cooled, remove them from the water and dry them on paper towels.

7. Take 1 strip of prosciutto and roll it around 1 gnocchi. Secure the roll by inserting a toothpick half in it. Repeat for all of the gnocchi and prosciutto.

8. Place enough olive oil in a large sauté pan to lightly coat the bottom, and heat it over medium-high heat. Add the gnocchi to the pan and cook on all sides until the prosciutto is crispy, about 30 seconds per side. When the prosciutto is cooked, place the gnocchi on a plate lined with paper towels to drain.

9. Remove the toothpicks, arrange on a platter, and serve warm.

Wild Mushroom Risotto Bites

MAKES 20

WILD MUSHROOM RISOTTO IS transformed here into a convenient bite-size dish. While shiitakes are most commonly available, I also use hedgehog and blue foot mushrooms. Use what you can find most readily—even dried mushrooms reconstituted in warm water. Whatever kinds you use, the amount should equal about three fourths of a cup once chopped.
❋ I use poha, Indian rice flakes, to bread these risotto balls—an idea I got from chef Floyd Cardoz at Tabla in New York. If you can't find poha at an Indian store, use panko, Japanese breadcrumbs, instead.

6 ounces total shiitake and/or other wild mushrooms, stemmed
Olive oil
2 garlic cloves, cut in half
3 sprigs thyme
3 sprigs rosemary
Fine sea salt
Freshly ground white pepper
2½ cups chicken stock
¼ cup minced onion
1 cup Arborio rice
¼ cup dry white wine
2 tablespoons mascarpone
1 large egg yolk, beaten
1 quart canola oil, for frying
2 large egg whites, lightly whipped
1½ cups poha or panko
White truffle oil

1. Wash each kind of mushroom separately in cold water. Dry the mushrooms well on paper towels. Heat enough olive oil in a large sauté pan to coat the bottom, and heat it over medium-high heat. Add 1 piece of garlic, 1 sprig of thyme, 1 sprig of rosemary, and the shiitakes. Sauté until all their liquid has evaporated and the pan is dry. Season them with salt and pepper. Transfer them to a bowl, let cool slightly, and then chop fine. Repeat with the other kinds of mushrooms, using a piece of garlic and a sprig of each herb each time.

2. Bring the chicken stock to a boil and season it well with salt and pepper. Keep the stock at a low simmer.

3. Place enough olive oil in a large sauté pan to coat the bottom, and heat it over medium-high heat. Add the onion and cook until it is translucent, about 4 minutes. Add the rice and stir until it is coated with the oil. Add the white wine and let it reduce until the pan is almost dry. When the wine has reduced, begin adding the hot chicken stock, about ¼ cup at a time, stirring constantly. Let each addition of stock be absorbed by the rice before you add the next. This will take 20 to 25 minutes in all. The rice should be very well cooked. Transfer the cooked risotto to a bowl and let it cool slightly. When it is warm rather than hot, mix in the mascarpone, egg yolk, and chopped mushrooms. Adjust the seasoning with salt and pepper.

4. Fill a medium saucepan with the canola oil. Clip a deep-frying thermometer to the side of the pan, and heat the oil to 350° F.

5. Roll the risotto mixture with your hands into 20 equal balls, each about the size of a large melon ball. Place the egg whites and rice flakes in separate shallow containers. Dip the risotto balls, a few at a time, into the egg whites (shaking off any excess) and then into the rice flakes, coating them thoroughly.

6. When all of the risotto balls are coated, fry them, a few at a time, until golden brown, about 4 minutes. Do not crowd the pan, and maintain the oil at a steady 350° F. As they are done, remove the risotto balls from the oil and place them on a plate lined with paper towels to drain. Sprinkle with salt.

7. The risotto balls may be served immediately or kept at room temperature for 2 to 3 hours and then warmed in a 300° to 350° F oven for 5 minutes. Just before serving, place a small drop of white truffle oil on each one. Arrange on a platter, and serve warm.

CHEESE

Cheese platters are easy to put together but are not very original, so I prefer to use cheese as one ingredient in small bites. Serve one or two per party, depending on the other dishes on your menu. Feel free to substitute your favorites, but do stay within the cheese family suggested. Comté or Emmental can replace Gruyère, for example, but will have a milder taste, and Raclette or a soft Tomme can be substituted for Reblochon.

Cherry Tomatoes Filled with Goat Cheese

Here is an easy small bite, perfect in summer when tomatoes are at their best. Goat cheese, tomatoes, scallions, and basil come together in an explosion of freshness.

❊ If you can find them, use baby tomatoes grown on the vine with their stems still attached; the presentation is stunning. But it is just as delicious with cherry or grape tomatoes, which are easier to obtain.

20 large cherry tomatoes

8 ounces fresh goat cheese

2 tablespoons extra virgin olive oil

1 scallion, white and green parts, thinly sliced on the diagonal

1 tablespoon basil chiffonade (see Note)

½ tablespoon chopped tarragon

½ tablespoon cracked black peppercorns

Fine sea salt

1. Cut off the top of each tomato with a sharp knife, taking care to keep the stems, if any, attached. Set the tops aside. Using a small melon baller, scoop out and discard the tomato pulp.

2. In a bowl, whisk the goat cheese and olive oil together until the mixture is smooth. Stir in the scallion, basil, tarragon, and black pepper. Season with salt. Place the cheese mixture in a plastic pastry bag or a resealable plastic bag, and cut a ¼-inch opening in the tip or corner. You can prepare the cheese a few hours before your party and keep it refrigerated, but it is best to place it in the bag and pipe it shortly before serving.

3. Season the inside of each tomato with salt. Pipe enough of the cheese mixture into each tomato so that the filling is just coming out of the top. Replace the tomato tops, and arrange on a platter.

NOTE: To make a basil chiffonade, place the leaves on top of one another to make a little pile. Roll the pile tightly, then cut it crosswise in very thin slices.

Greek Salad Brochettes

MAKES 20

THESE SKEWERS PACK A LOT of flavors into just one bite. Serving Greek salad on skewers makes them party-friendly, since there is no need for plates and forks.

2 tablespoons extra virgin olive oil

1 tablespoon chopped dill

Fine sea salt

Freshly ground white pepper

1 large cucumber, peeled, seeded, and cut into ½-inch squares

20 Kalamata olives, pitted

Twenty ¼-inch cubes of feta

4 romaine heart leaves, cut into ½-inch squares on the rib

1. Place the olive oil and dill in a small bowl. Mix to combine, and season with salt and pepper.

2. On a skewer, assemble 1 cucumber cube, 1 olive, 1 feta cube, and 1 romaine square. Brush the dill mixture over the vegetables. Repeat with the remaining ingredients to make 20 brochettes.

3. Arrange on a serving platter, and serve at room temperature.

Roquefort Mousse with Port Gelée, Walnuts, and Pears

MAKES ENOUGH FOR 20 SMALL GLASSES

T HIS TASTES AS IF YOU ARE eating cheese and drinking wine at once. As you dig a spoon into the layers, you encounter the sweet acidity of the port gelée, the freshness of the pear, the crunchiness of the walnut, and the softness of the mousse. Fill small glasses with the port gelée and prepare the mousse the night before. To give it time to soften, take the mousse out of the refrigerator ten to fifteen minutes before piping it into the glasses.

FOR THE PORT GELÉE:

3 cups port wine

1 3-inch-long cinnamon stick, cut or snapped in half

1 whole clove

1 piece orange peel, about 3 inches long and ½ inch wide

2 gelatin sheets, or 1 teaspoon (½ envelope) granulated gelatin

FOR THE MOUSSE:

8 ounces Roquefort, softened

½ cup crème fraîche or sour cream

Fine sea salt

Freshly ground white pepper

FOR THE GARNISH:

1 Anjou pear

20 walnut halves, toasted (see page 7)

1. Place the port, cinnamon stick, clove, and orange peel in a small pot over medium-high heat. Bring to a simmer and cook until the liquid reduces to 2 cups, about 5 minutes. Strain through a fine-mesh sieve into a bowl, and discard the cinnamon, clove, and orange peel.

2. Dissolve the gelatin sheets in the strained port and let it cool, but do not let it set, about 10 minutes. Arrange 20 shot glasses on a baking sheet to transfer in and out of the refrigerator. Fill ¼ inch of each shot glass with the port mixture, and refrigerate for 45 to 60 minutes to set.

3. Place the Roquefort and crème fraîche in a bowl, and whisk until the mixture is smooth. Season with salt and pepper. Fill a plastic pastry bag or a resealable plastic bag with the mousse and set aside.

4. Peel and core the pear, and then cut it into slices ⅛ inch wide and ½ inch long.

5. Once the gelée is firm, cut a ½-inch opening in the tip of the pastry bag or in the corner of the resealable bag. Fill each shot glass with about 2 teaspoons of the Roquefort mousse. Place a small mound of pear strips on top of the mousse and a walnut half on top. Arrange on a platter, and serve cold or at room temperature, with spoons.

Pea Purée and Ricotta Salata in Phyllo Cups

MAKES 20

THIS VERY LIGHT BITE combines the sweet taste of peas with the salty notes of ricotta salata, all enveloped in flaky phyllo dough. It's simple to put together, but you'd never guess that, based on the flavors it packs in. ❊ If you don't want to make phyllo cups, buy frozen ones.

2 cups fresh or frozen peas
2 tablespoons crème fraîche
¼ cup grated ricotta salata
Fine sea salt
Freshly ground white pepper
20 Phyllo Cups (page 8)
6-ounce piece of ricotta salata

1. Place a large pot of water over high heat and bring to a boil. Salt the boiling water, add the peas, and cook until done, 3 to 4 minutes for fresh peas and about 1 minute for frozen ones. Drain the peas and immediately place them in the bowl of a food processor. While the peas are still hot, purée until they are completely smooth. Pass the purée through a fine-mesh strainer into a bowl to remove the skins.

2. Place the purée, crème fraîche, and grated ricotta salata in a bowl and stir to combine completely. Season with salt and pepper.

3. Fill a pastry bag or a resealable plastic bag with the mixture. Cut a ½-inch opening in the tip or corner, and pipe it into the phyllo cups, filling them to the top. Grate the whole ricotta salata directly on top of the purée. Arrange on a platter, and serve at room temperature.

Tomato, Eggplant, and Goat Cheese Tarts

MAKES 20

TOMATO, EGGPLANT, AND GOAT cheese are classic ingredients from the South of France. They are often combined in a *tian*, which is a gratinéed vegetable casserole. The chutney here is the same as the one used for Lamb and Tomato Chutney on Cumin Wafers (page 152). For a more concentrated tomato flavor, pipe the filling into hollowed-out cherry tomatoes, or spread it on sautéed polenta rounds (page 47). Freeze any leftover dough.

One frozen puff pastry sheet (14 ounces), thawed in the refrigerator
2 tablespoons sherry vinegar
1 tablespoon lavender honey
2 tablespoons olive oil
2 Japanese eggplants, cut into ⅓-inch-thick slices
Fine sea salt
Freshly ground white pepper
3½ ounces fresh goat cheese
1 tablespoon chopped parsley
1 tablespoon chopped basil
1 recipe Tomato Chutney (see page 152)
20 small basil leaves

1. Preheat the oven to 400° F. Line a baking sheet with parchment paper.

2. On a lightly floured surface, roll the puff pastry out in all directions until it is ¼ inch thick. Cut out 20 rounds of dough with a 1¼-inch cookie cutter. Place the rounds on the prepared baking sheet, and place a wire rack over them (this will keep the rounds even and prevent them from rising too high). Bake for 20 minutes, or until light golden brown. Remove from the oven, take off the wire rack, and let the rounds cool on the baking sheet.

3. Mix the vinegar and honey together in a small bowl (to make it easier to mix, warm the honey by putting it in the microwave for 20 seconds). Heat the olive oil in a sauté pan over medium-high heat. Season the eggplant slices with salt and pepper. Add the eggplant to the pan and sauté on both sides until light brown, 1 minute per side. Add the honey mixture to the pan and cook to reduce it slightly, about 2 minutes.

4. Place the goat cheese, parsley, and chopped basil in the bowl of a food processor. Process until everything is well incorporated and the cheese takes a nice bright green color. Fill a plastic pastry bag or a resealable plastic bag with the cheese mixture and cut a ¼-inch opening in its tip or corner.

5. Spoon 1 teaspoon tomato chutney onto the center of each puff pastry round. Place 1 eggplant slice on top of the chutney, and pipe a dime-size amount of the cheese mixture over the eggplant. Garnish with a basil leaf. Arrange on a platter, and serve at room temperature.

Ratatouille in Parmesan Cups

MAKES 20

RATATOUILLE IS A TRADITIONAL vegetable dish from Provence, in the South of France. It's a perfect showcase for tomatoes, zucchini, eggplants, and bell peppers at the height of summer, since it really lets their flavors come through without much more than the support of olive oil. Do not stir the vegetables too vigorously when you cook them, or they will turn into an unappetizing mush. Bake the Parmesan cups in small batches, because if they cool before they are molded, they will harden and you will be unable to shape them. All the vegetables should be cut the same size so that they cook evenly.

1¼ cups grated Parmesan
Olive oil
½ cup diced red onion
1 garlic clove, minced
½ cup diced red bell pepper, peeled
½ cup diced yellow bell pepper, peeled
¾ cup diced peeled eggplant
½ cup diced zucchini
2 beefsteak tomatoes, peeled, seeded (see page 6), and diced
3 tablespoons chopped basil
Fine sea salt
Freshly ground white pepper

1. Preheat the oven to 400° F. Line a baking sheet with a Silpat.

2. Spread 1 tablespoon of the Parmesan in a 2-inch round on the Silpat. Repeat to form 5 or 6 rounds. Place the baking sheet in the oven and bake for about 5 minutes, or until the Parmesan begins to bubble and turns a light golden brown. Remove from the oven and let the Parmesan cool for 1 minute. Then lift the rounds from the Silpat and place them in the cups of a mini-muffin pan to form a cup shape. Let the Parmesan cool and harden for 3 to 4 minutes. When they are cool, gently twist the cups out of the molds and line them up on a flat surface. It is better to not pile them up. Repeat with the remaining Parmesan to make 20 cups.

3. Place enough olive oil in a large pot to coat the bottom, and heat it over medium-high heat. Add the onion, garlic, and the red and yellow peppers and cook until halfway done, about 3 minutes. Add the eggplant and zucchini and cook for another 3 minutes. Add the tomatoes and cook until most of the moisture has evaporated, 3 minutes. Add the basil, and season with salt and pepper.

4. Fill each Parmesan cup with the ratatouille. Arrange on a platter, and serve warm.

Gougères

THIS IS MY FATHER'S RECIPE—the best cheese puffs you've ever tasted. Gougères are best served warm, so pipe them at the last minute and bake them just before your guests arrive. Freeze any leftover baked gougères in a tightly sealed plastic bag for up to a month. Warm them up before serving by placing them in a 350°F oven for three to four minutes.

6 tablespoons (¾ stick) unsalted butter
3½ cups plus 2 tablespoons all-purpose flour, sifted
Pinch of salt
Pinch of cayenne pepper
Pinch of freshly ground nutmeg
5 large eggs
5 ounces (½ cup plus 2 tablespoons) heavy cream, slightly heated so it is warm to the touch
3½ cups grated Gruyère, plus more for garnish if desired

1. Preheat the oven to 400° F. Line a baking sheet with parchment paper.

2. Place 1 cup water and the butter in a medium saucepan over medium-high heat and bring to a boil. Then reduce the heat to low and add the flour, salt, cayenne, and nutmeg. Cook the mixture for 15 to 20 minutes, stirring constantly, until it turns into a thick paste and no longer sticks to the sides of the pan.

3. Transfer the batter to the bowl of an electric mixer fitted with the paddle attachment. Mix at low speed, incorporating the eggs one at a time. Do not add an egg until the previous one is completely incorporated.

4. Add the cream to the batter while the mixer is running. Then stop the mixer and gently stir in the grated Gruyère with a spatula, making sure not to deflate the dough.

5. Fit a pastry bag with a #5 or ½-inch star tip, and fill it with the dough. Pipe 1-inch rounds of the dough onto the prepared baking sheet. Wet your finger and smooth out the top of the gougères. Bake for 10 to 15 minutes, until golden brown.

6. Remove from the oven and sprinkle grated Gruyère on top if desired. Arrange on a platter, and serve warm.

Morel Ragoût in Gorgonzola Cream

MUSHROOMS AND CREAM SAUCE are a classic combination. Adding Gorgonzola makes this dish even more delicious. If you have particularly large morels, or if you are substituting a different, larger type of mushroom, chop them into ¼-inch pieces before cooking so they will fit on the toasts. Use dried morels reconstituted in warm water or fresh chanterelles, and a regular baguette instead of a ficelle if you prefer.

1 baguette or ficelle, cut diagonally into 20 slices ¼ inch thick and 1½ inches long
Olive oil
1 quart canola oil, for frying
20 baby spinach leaves
Fleur de sel

FOR THE RAGOÛT:
10 ounces morels
Olive oil
2 tablespoons minced shallots
1 cup heavy cream
4 ounces Gorgonzola, crumbled
Fine sea salt
Freshly ground white pepper

1. Preheat the oven to 400° F.

2. Place the bread slices in a single layer on a baking sheet and drizzle with olive oil. Toast in the oven for about 8 minutes, until golden brown. Remove from the oven and leave on the baking sheet until ready to serve.

3. Fill a medium saucepan with the canola oil. Clip a deep-frying thermometer to the side of the pan, and heat the oil to 350° F.

4. Deep-fry the spinach leaves in small batches, leaving them in the oil for 10 to 15 seconds. Do not crowd the pan, and maintain the oil at a steady 350° F. When they are done, remove the leaves from the oil with a slotted spoon and place them on a plate lined with paper towels to drain. Sprinkle with salt.

5. Clean the morels to make sure that they are free of dirt and bugs, and cut them into ¼-inch pieces if necessary. Place enough olive oil in a wide pot to coat the bottom, and heat it over medium heat. Add the shallots and cook without browning for 2 to 3 minutes. Add the morels and raise the heat to medium-high. Cook until the morels release their juices and begin to soften. Add the cream, raise the heat to high, and cook until the liquid has reduced by three-fourths, 5 to 6 minutes. Whisk in the crumbled Gorgonzola, and season with salt and pepper.

6. Place ½ tablespoon of the mushroom ragoût on each toast. Garnish with a small pinch of fleur de sel and a fried spinach leaf. Arrange on a serving platter, and serve warm.

Fried Artichokes with Reblochon

MAKES 20

REBLOCHON, A CREAMY, SOFT-RIND cheese from the Savoie region of eastern France, goes well with artichokes. Baby artichokes, which are plentiful from March to May, have less fuzz than large artichokes, making them easier to prepare. You can also make this dish year-round with the oil-packed baby artichokes.

Juice of 1 lemon
20 baby artichokes
Olive oil
2 garlic cloves, crushed
4 thyme sprigs
8 ounces Reblochon
2 quarts canola oil, for frying
¾ cup all-purpose flour
4 large eggs, lightly beaten
2 cups dried breadcrumbs
Fine sea salt
Freshly ground white pepper

1. Add the lemon juice to 1 quart water in a large nonreactive bowl. Peel off the outer leaves of the artichokes, and trim the bottoms. Cut off the tough outer green parts of the stem and around the bottom of the artichokes until just the heart is left. Using a melon baller, remove the inside of the artichoke, cleaning it thoroughly of its fuzzy center. As you work your way through the artichokes, keep the hollowed ones in the lemon water to prevent them from turning brown. When they are all ready, remove the artichokes from the lemon water and dry them well on a kitchen towel.

2. Place enough olive oil in a medium saucepan to cover the bottom, and heat it over medium heat. Cut out a round of parchment paper the same size as the pan. Add the garlic and thyme to the pan, and then the artichokes. (Cook in two batches if they don't all fit.) Add 2 cups water and place the parchment round directly over the artichokes. Cook for 6 minutes. Then remove the artichokes from the pan and dry them on a kitchen towel. Stuff each artichoke with 1 heaping teaspoon of the Reblochon.

3. Fill a medium saucepan with the canola oil. Clip a deep-frying thermometer to the side of the pan, and heat the oil to 350° F.

4. Place the flour, eggs, and breadcrumbs in separate shallow containers. Season the flour and the breadcrumbs with salt and pepper. Roll the stuffed artichokes in the flour, then the eggs (shaking off the excess), and then the breadcrumbs, coating them well.

5. Fry the artichokes, a few at a time, until golden brown, 3 to 4 minutes. Do not crowd the pan, and maintain the oil at a steady 350° F. As they are cooked, remove the artichokes to a plate lined with paper towels and sprinkle lightly with salt. Arrange on a platter, and serve warm.

Cheese Sticks

MAKES 20

THIS IS MY FAVORITE SNACK to eat in front of the television. Many store-bought cheese sticks are too hard; these are crisp on the outside, yet soft on the inside. Bake the sticks when you have a few scraps of leftover puff pastry to use—they may not be perfectly shaped, but they'll be just as good. Freeze any leftover dough, tightly wrapped in plastic wrap, for up to a month.

One frozen puff pastry sheet (14 ounces), thawed in the refrigerator
1 cup grated Parmesan
1 tablespoon paprika
Freshly ground black pepper

1. Preheat the oven to 400° F. Line a baking sheet with parchment paper.

2. Roll the puff pastry out in all directions to form a rectangle that is ⅛ inch thick. Sprinkle with the Parmesan, paprika, and pepper. Cut with a pizza wheel into ¼-inch-wide, 5-inch-long strips.

3. Place the puff pastry strips on the prepared baking sheet and bake for 20 minutes, or until lightly browned. Remove from the oven and let cool slightly before arranging in a tall vessel or on a platter. Serve slightly warm or at room temperature.

SEE THE PHOTOGRAPH ON PAGE 53

FISH AND SHELLFISH

Seafood hors d'oeuvres are the ones most requested for the parties we cater. Vary the selection of the fish dishes you offer, playing with textures, types, and cooking methods. From raw to fried, from shrimp to monkfish, most of these recipes can be made with seafood from your supermarket. Befriend the market's fishmonger. He can help you with special orders and ensure that you always get the freshest fish. This is particularly important for the raw fish dishes, such as sushi, tartares, and ceviches.

Scallop Ceviche with Grapefruit Gelée

MAKES 20

T O KEEP THIS DISH CHILLED during the course of a party, place the scallop shells or spoons on a tray covered with crushed ice sprinkled with rock salt. You can also fill your tray or serving platter with just rock salt or with seaweed; the latter can be found at the fish market. These won't keep the ceviche chilled, but if you do not plan on letting it sit out for hours, it will not be an issue. ❀ This dish can be prepared six to eight hours before serving. You can buy decorative 2½-inch-wide scallop shells, or serve the ceviche in Chinese soupspoons.

3 grapefruits
Juice of 1 lemon
1 celery stalk, finely diced
1 cucumber, finely diced
½ red onion, finely diced
1 garlic clove, very finely minced
Fine sea salt
Freshly ground white pepper
60 bay scallops
2 teaspoons (1 envelope) unflavored gelatin

1. Juice 2 of the grapefruits into a bowl. Segment the third (see page 6). Cut the segments into ⅛-inch cubes, and reserve.

2. In a large bowl, mix half the grapefruit juice with the lemon juice, celery, cucumber, onion, and garlic. Season with salt and pepper. Add the scallops and grapefruit segment

3. Place the remaining grapefruit juice in a small saucepan and sprinkle the gelatin over it. Let it sit for 4 to 5 minutes. Then bring the juice to a simmer over medium-low heat to dissolve the gelatin. Remove it from the heat and let it cool to room temperature.

4. Add the cooled gelée to the scallop mixture. Mix lightly to ensure that everything is coated with the gelatin.

5. If you are using scallop shells, crumple aluminum foil and place it on a baking sheet. Set 20 scallop shells on the baking sheet, securing them in the crumpled foil so that they don't tip. If you are using Chinese soupspoons, which have a flat bottom, you don't need the foil.

6. Divide the scallop mixture among the shells or soupspoons, and refrigerate until the gelatin has set and is firm to the touch, about 1 hour.

7. Right before serving, remove the shells or spoons from the refrigerator and arrange them on a tray. Serve chilled.

Crab and Mango Salad in Apple Cups

MAKES 20

THIS IS A VERY FRESH, light bite, perfect when apples make their first appearance in the early autumn. ❀ You can also serve this salad in Phyllo Cups (page 8) or on store-bought apple chips.

FOR THE CUPS:
¼ cup sugar
1 Golden Delicious apple

FOR THE DRESSING:
1 Golden Delicious apple
2 teaspoons coarsely chopped shallot
1 teaspoon chopped garlic
⅔ cup olive oil
2 tablespoons cider vinegar
Fine sea salt
Freshly ground white pepper

FOR THE SALAD:
1 mango
1 Golden Delicious apple
1 pound crabmeat, picked over for shells and cartilage
2 tablespoons chopped cilantro
Fine sea salt
Freshly ground white pepper

FOR THE GARNISH:
1 Golden Delicious apple

1. Preheat the oven to 180° F. Line a baking sheet with a Silpat.

2. Place the sugar and 1 cup water in a saucepan over medium-high heat, and boil until the sugar dissolves, about 1 to 2 minutes. Remove the sugar syrup from the heat and let it cool to room temperature.

3. Slice the whole, uncored apple horizontally into paper-thin slices (the thinner the slices are, the faster they will dry). Dip the slices into the sugar syrup, and lay them flat on the prepared baking sheet.

4. Place the baking sheet in the oven and bake for 2 to 2½ hours, until the apple slices are dry and firm but still bend slightly.

5. While the chips are still warm and pliable, press them into the cups of a mini-muffin pan (or a Flexipan mold with 1-inch-deep cups), to shape them into cups. If the chips cool and become too hard to remove from the Silpat or to bend into a cup shape, warm them for a minute or two in the oven to soften them.

6. Make the dressing: Peel and core the apple, and chop it into medium pieces. Place the apple pieces, shallot, garlic, olive oil, and vinegar in a blender and pulse until everything is puréed and emulsified like a vinaigrette. Season with salt and pepper.

7. Make the salad: Peel the mango and cut the flesh away from the core. Cut the flesh into ¼-inch cubes. Peel and core the apple, and cut it into

¼-inch cubes. Mix the crabmeat, mango, apple, and cilantro together in a bowl. Add the dressing, stir, and season to taste with salt and pepper.

8. Make the garnish: Peel and core the apple, and cut it into long, thin strips.

9. Place ½ tablespoon of the salad in each of the apple cups. Garnish with an apple strip. Arrange on a platter, and serve immediately.

Citrus-Cured Salmon Gravlax with Vegetable Relish

MAKES 20

GRAVLAX IS A CURING PROCESS that preserves the fish. Once you remove the salmon from the cure, it will keep for two days in the refrigerator. I use celery leaves for decoration, but dill or flat-leaf parsley also works well.

FOR THE GRAVLAX:
12 ounces salmon fillet, skin removed
⅓ cup coarse sea salt
½ cup sugar
2 tablespoons chopped mint
2 tablespoons chopped dill
2 tablespoons chopped tarragon
Grated zest of 1 orange
Grated zest of 2 lemons
Grated zest of 2 limes

FOR THE VEGETABLE RELISH:
¼ cup finely diced peeled cucumber
¼ cup finely diced celery
¼ cup finely diced red onion
¼ cup finely diced peeled red bell pepper
¼ cup finely diced peeled, seeded tomato (see page 6)
1 tablespoon capers, drained and rinsed
2 anchovy fillets, minced
2 garlic cloves, minced
½ teaspoon crushed red pepper flakes
Juice of 2 lemons
⅓ cup red wine vinegar
1 cup extra virgin olive oil
Fine sea salt
Freshly ground white pepper
1 tablespoon chopped thyme
1 tablespoon chopped chives
1 tablespoon chopped cilantro
8 basil leaves, cut in chiffonade (see Note, page 54)

FOR THE GARNISH:
20 celery leaves (optional)

1. Line an 8-inch square cake pan or a baking sheet with parchment paper, and cut a second sheet of parchment to the same size.

2. Cut the salmon lengthwise into 2-inch-wide pieces. In a bowl, mix the sea salt, sugar, mint, dill, tarragon, and citrus zests.

3. Place the salmon in the prepared pan. Spread half of the sea salt mixture over the salmon. Turn the salmon over and spread the remaining mixture over it, covering it completely. Place the second sheet of parchment on top of the fish and wrap it tightly. The fish should be tightly encased between the two sheets of parchment to ensure proper curing. Refrigerate for 72 hours, turning it over after 36 hours.

4. In a bowl, mix the cucumber, celery, red onion, bell pepper, tomato, capers, anchovies, garlic, crushed red pepper, lemon juice, red wine vinegar, and olive oil. Season with salt and pepper. Stir in the thyme, chives, cilantro, and basil. Refrigerate, covered, for at least 2 hours to allow the vegetables to marinate.

5. Remove the salmon from the refrigerator. Wipe off all of the sea salt mixture. Slice the salmon at a 45-degree angle, forming strips 1 inch wide and 2 inches long. Roll each strip up.

6. Strain any excess liquid from the vegetable relish. Place ½ tablespoon of the relish in a Chinese soupspoon, and place a piece of rolled salmon on top of the relish. Repeat, filling 20 spoons in all. Garnish each spoon with a celery leaf if desired, and serve.

Salmon Tartare in Radish Cups

MAKES 20

THE SPICY RADISHES BALANCE the richness of the salmon. Another presentation idea is to serve the tartare in Chinese soupspoons: finely dice the radishes and toss them with the salmon.

10 large radishes
8 ounces salmon fillet, skin on
Olive oil
¼ teaspoon Asian sesame oil
Fine sea salt
Freshly ground white pepper

1. Cut a small slice off the top and bottom of each radish. Then cut each radish in half cross-wise. Using a small melon baller, hollow out the center of each radish, making a cup about ⅛ inch deep.

2. Remove the skin from the salmon in one piece. Place enough olive oil in a sauté pan to coat the bottom, and heat it over high heat. Sauté the salmon skin in the pan until it becomes crispy, about 2 minutes. The skin has a tendency to curl up, so press it down with a spatula. Remove the skin from the pan and reserve.

3. Cut the salmon flesh into very small cubes, and place them in a bowl. Add the sesame oil, season with salt and pepper, and toss to mix.

4. Fill the radish cups with the salmon tartare. Break off a small piece of the crispy salmon skin and use it to garnish the top of each radish cup. You can prepare these in the morning, place them over crushed ice, and keep them in the refrigerator.

5. Arrange the radishes on a platter, and serve cold.

Lime Salmon on Potato Crisps

MAKES 20

T HIS DISH IS LIKE EATING SALMON sashimi on a potato chip. To get really thin potato slices, use a mandoline. The chip has to be thin enough not to overpower the taste of the salmon, yet sturdy enough to withstand the weight of the fish. If you don't want to make your own chips, use a good store-bought brand that is not too oily or salty, such as Terra Chips.

FOR THE SALMON:

Grated zest and juice of 2 limes
¼ cup extra virgin olive oil
Pinch of salt
Freshly ground white pepper
1 pound salmon, skin removed

FOR THE POTATO CRISPS:

1 quart canola oil, for frying
2 large Idaho potatoes
Fine sea salt

FOR THE GARNISH:

1 lime, segmented (see page 6)
1 tablespoon finely chopped chives
1 tablespoon fleur de sel

1. Place the lime zest and juice in a small bowl. Stir in the olive oil, and season with salt and pepper.

2. Line a small baking sheet with parchment paper. Cut the salmon crosswise into 3 wide pieces, 1 to 1½ inches long. Slice each piece lengthwise into ¹⁄₁₆-inch-wide strips. Place the salmon strips in a single layer on the prepared baking sheet. With a small pastry brush, generously brush the lime marinade over the sliced salmon. Roll each salmon strip into a little spiral. Cover and refrigerate for 2 hours.

3. Fill a medium saucepan with the canola oil. Clip a deep-frying thermometer to the side of the pan, and heat the oil to 300° F.

4. Cut the potatoes into rectangles 2½ inches long, 1 inch wide, and 1 inch thick. Slice the rectangles lengthwise into ¹⁄₁₆-inch-thick pieces. Pat them dry.

5. Fry the potato slices, a few at a time, until they are a light golden brown, 3 to 4 minutes. Do not crowd the pan, and maintain the oil at a steady 300° F. As they are done, remove the potato crisps from the oil and place them on a plate lined with paper towels to drain. Sprinkle with salt. You can make these a few hours ahead.

6. Dice the lime segments into ⅛-inch cubes. Place a salmon roll on top of a potato crisp. Sprinkle with chives and fleur de sel. Place a piece of diced lime on top of the salmon. Repeat with the remaining salmon, potato crisps, and garnish. Arrange on a platter, and serve cold.

Kumamoto Oysters with Yuzu Sorbet and Caviar

MAKES 20

YUZU IS A MEDIUM-SIZE JAPANESE citrus fruit with an aromatic rind. Its flesh and juice are very sour. Yuzus are hard to find in the U.S., but the bottled juice can be found in gourmet markets. Select the unsalted variety. The sorbet can also be made with other citrus juices, such as calamansi, orange, grapefruit, or lemon juice. Kumamotos are small West Coast oysters. You can substitute any oyster you prefer in this sophisticated pairing. ❋ To keep the oysters and the sorbet chilled, put a layer of crushed ice on your platter. Cover the ice with some rock salt to prevent it from melting too fast, and set the oysters on top.

¼ cup sugar
1 large egg white, beaten until frothy
1 cup yuzu juice
20 Kumamoto oysters
1 tablespoon American paddlefish caviar

1. Place the sugar and 1 cup water in a small saucepan over medium-high heat. Bring to a boil and stir until all of the sugar has dissolved, about 2 minutes.

2. Transfer the sugar syrup to a bowl and let it cool slightly. Then refrigerate until it is completely chilled, about 1 hour.

3. Mix the egg white, yuzu juice, and chilled sugar syrup in a bowl. Pour the mixture into an ice cream maker and process according to the manufacturer's instructions.

4. Once the sorbet is ready, either use it immediately or place it in a lidded container and store it in the freezer for up to 3 days.

5. Shuck the oysters with an oyster knife, holding them securely in a towel (see page 7). Place a small scoop of the sorbet on top of each oyster. Top with a few grains of caviar. Arrange on a platter, and serve immediately.

Monkfish Mousse with Tomato Gelée and Salsa

MAKES 20

THIS DISH IS ALMOST LIKE a Bavarian cream, a firm mousse-based dessert. The firmness here comes from the tomato gelée, while the salsa brings freshness and contrasting texture. If you can't find monkfish, use any type of whitefish, such as halibut or cod, but don't forget to remove the skin (monkfish is sold skinless). ❋ Start this dish the night before so the gelée can set, or even two days ahead, but wait until the day you plan to serve the dish before preparing the mousse and the salsa.

FOR THE TOMATO GELÉE:

10 tomatoes, peeled and seeded (see page 6)
2 teaspoons (1 envelope) unflavored gelatin
1 tablespoon tomato paste
Fine sea salt
Freshly ground white pepper

FOR THE MOUSSE:

2 cups whole milk
10 ounces monkfish fillet
½ cup heavy cream
Fine sea salt
Freshly ground white pepper

FOR THE SALSA:

6 plum tomatoes, peeled, seeded (see page 6), and diced

¼ cup diced red onion
1 jalapeño pepper, seeded and finely diced
1 tablespoon chopped cilantro
Juice of 1 lime
Fine sea salt
Freshly ground white pepper

1. Make the tomato gelée: Place the tomatoes in a blender and purée until smooth. Place a clean linen towel over the top of a tall container, letting the middle of the towel hang slightly below the rim of the container. Secure the towel to the container by placing a rubber band around it. Pour the puréed tomatoes into the center of the towel, so the juice is strained into the container. Refrigerate the container, with the draining purée, overnight or for at least 8 hours.

2. The next day, discard the tomato pulp left in the towel. Place the strained tomato juice in a small pot and sprinkle the gelatin over it. Let it sit for 4 to 5 minutes. Then stir in the tomato paste and bring to a simmer over medium heat to dissolve the gelatin. Season with salt and pepper. Then remove it from the heat and transfer the mixture to a bowl. Chill it in the refrigerator until cool, about 15 minutes. Do not let it become firm.

3. Place 20 shot or cordial glasses on a baking sheet (to make it easier to transfer them in and out of the refrigerator). Fill each of the glasses one third of the way up with about 2 tablespoons of the cooled (but still liquid) gelée. Refrigerate until the tomato gelée sets completely, about 1 hour, or up to 1 day.

4. Heat the milk to a simmer in a medium pot over medium-high heat. Add the monkfish and poach until cooked, 3 to 4 minutes. Remove it to a plate and let it cool. Discard the milk.

5. Remove any stray bones from the fish and place it in the bowl of a food processor. Blend until smooth. Pour the monkfish purée into a fine-mesh sieve set over a bowl. Using a spatula, press the purée through the sieve (this will give it a smooth consistency).

6. Whip the cream until it forms soft peaks. Fold the whipped cream into the monkfish purée, and season with salt and pepper.

7. Place the monkfish mousse in a plastic pastry bag or a resealable plastic bag, and cut a ¾-inch opening in the tip or corner. Pipe the monkfish mousse on top of the tomato gelée, filling each glass by another third. Refrigerate until ready to serve.

8. Mix the diced tomatoes, red onion, jalapeño, cilantro, and lime juice in a bowl. Season with salt and pepper.

9. When ready to serve, remove the shot glasses from the refrigerator and place ½ tablespoon tomato salsa on top of the monkfish mousse in each one. Arrange on a platter, and serve with spoons.

Tuna Tartare in Sesame Cones

MAKES 20

MANY OF OUR CATERING clients request one of our savory cones filled with fish—tuna tartare, salmon rillettes, or smoked trout rillettes—because they are real showstoppers. Fortunately the cones are actually quite easy to make. Use cone-shaped molds if you have them, or make your own molds as explained on page 8. For a unique presentation, gently stand the cones in a decorative bowl filled with three inches of rice, dried beans, lentils, red peppercorns, coriander seeds, or other spices. ❀ Sesame oil is very strong, so use it sparingly. Two drops might seem like a small amount, but it is more than enough. I typically use a French sesame oil, which is harder to find, so use the Asian variety if that's all you can get. ❀ *Ponzu* is a Japanese sauce consisting of an acidic component, like lemon juice or vinegar, mixed with bonito flakes and seaweed; you will find it in the international foods section of your supermarket, near the miso. Refrigerate both after opening. ❀ Work quickly to shape the cones, and make a few extra in case one breaks. You can also shape the tuiles on a rolling pin if don't want to make cones.

FOR THE SESAME CONES:

3 tablespoons light corn syrup
½ teaspoon red miso
½ teaspoon ground ginger
2 drops French or Asian sesame oil
¼ cup pastry flour, sifted
½ tablespoon unsalted butter, softened
2 teaspoons white sesame seeds
2 teaspoons black sesame seeds

FOR THE MISO DRESSING:

3 tablespoons ponzu
2 tablespoons lemon juice
1 tablespoon sweet (white) miso
1 cup extra virgin olive oil

FOR THE TUNA TARTARE:

7 ounces sushi-grade tuna, skin, bones, and sinews removed, diced very fine
1 tablespoon finely diced peeled red bell pepper
1 tablespoon finely diced red onion
1 teaspoon finely diced jalapeño pepper
Fine sea salt
Freshly ground white pepper

1. Preheat the oven to 400° F. Line a baking sheet with a Silpat.

2. In a mixing bowl, combine the corn syrup, red miso, ginger, and sesame oil. In a separate bowl, blend the pastry flour with the butter. Combine the flour-butter mixture with the miso mixture, and then stir in the sesame seeds. Using an off-set spatula, spread a thin layer of the sesame batter on the prepared baking sheet, forming a round approximately 2½ inches in diameter. Make about 8 rounds on the Silpat. Bake for 4 to 5 minutes, until the sesame batter turns a golden brown color. Remove the pan from the

oven and allow the tuiles to cool slightly, 2 to 3 minutes. Be careful, because they become hard quickly and then are impossible to shape.

3. To shape a tuile into a cone, wrap it around the tip of a cone-shaped mold and lay it on its side on a wire rack. This must be done while the sesame tuiles are still warm and pliable; if a tuile becomes too crisp to wrap around the mold, place it back in the oven for a minute to soften. Once the cones have cooled and hardened, gently twist them off the molds and lay them back down on a baking sheet or a large plate.

4. Repeat this baking and shaping process until you have 20 small sesame cones. Let them sit at room temperature while you prepare the filling.

5. In a small bowl, mix the ponzu, lemon juice, and sweet miso together. Then slowly whisk in the olive oil to incorporate. In a separate bowl, mix the tuna with the bell pepper, onion, and jalapeño. Season the tuna mixture with 3 table-spoons of the miso dressing and some salt and pepper. Refrigerate until ready to serve.

6. Just before serving, fill a pastry bag or a resealable plastic bag with the tuna mixture and cut a ½-inch opening in the tip or corner. Pipe a small amount of tuna tartare into each cone. Arrange the cones in a deep tray or dish filled with rice or lentils, and serve.

Salmon Rillettes Cones

MAKES 20

THIS IS PAYARD EXECUTIVE CHEF Philippe Bertineau's recipe for salmon rillettes—rillettes being a preparation in which a fish or meat is cooked very slowly and then ground and made into a spread. The *brik* dough called for is like a thick, sturdier phyllo (which is too fragile to shape into cones); it is easy to work with because it does not dry out the way phyllo does. It is sometimes called *feuilles de brik*, *pâte à brik*, or even *brick*. See Resources (page 167) for purchasing information. You can also serve the rillettes on crackers, potato chips, or small bites of French or pumpernickel bread.

FOR THE CONES:
10 sheets brik dough
2 large egg whites, lightly beaten
2 tablespoons poppy seeds

FOR THE RILLETTES:
1 cup dry white wine
1 shallot, minced
1 thyme sprig
1 rosemary sprig
8 ounces salmon fillet, skin removed, cut into ½-inch cubes
2 ounces smoked salmon, diced small
Grated zest of 1 lemon
2 tablespoons mayonnaise
Fine sea salt
Freshly ground white pepper

FOR THE GARNISH:
20 small dill sprigs

1. Preheat the oven to 400° F. Place a wire rack over a baking sheet. Spray 20 cone-shaped molds with cooking spray.

2. With a small knife, trace an 8-inch circle on a sheet of brik dough (use an 8-inch round cake pan to trace around). Cut out the round, then cut it in half. Repeat with the remaining sheets of brik. Brush each half-round with some of the beaten egg whites. Place the flat edge of the half-round vertically on a cone mold, about 1 inch down from its wider opening. The flat edge should fall straight down the mold, as a continuation of its pointed tip. Hold the flat edge securely to the mold, and roll the mold over the curved edge of the dough to create a cone. Repeat with the remaining brik and molds.

3. Sprinkle the cones with poppy seeds (if the dough becomes dry, brush it again with some of the egg whites to help the poppy seeds stick). Lay the cones flat on the wire rack and bake for 8 to 10 minutes, or until they are golden brown. Remove from the oven and let cool. When the cones are cool, gently twist them off the molds. You can make these up to 2 days ahead and keep them in a tightly sealed container.

4. Place the wine, shallot, thyme, and rosemary in a saucepan over high heat, and bring to a boil. Turn it down to a low simmer and add the salmon fillet. Poach until the salmon is cooked, about 4 minutes. Discard the thyme and rosemary, and drain the salmon well. Allow it to cool. Place the cooled salmon in a bowl and crush it with a fork. Refrigerate until completely chilled, about 30 minutes.

5. Add the smoked salmon, lemon zest, and mayonnaise to the chilled salmon, and stir to combine. Season with salt and pepper.

6. To assemble, fill a plastic pastry bag or a resealable plastic bag with the salmon rillettes. Cut a ¾-inch opening in the tip or corner, and squeeze a small amount of rillette into each cone. Place a small dill sprig on top of each cone. Serve in a cone tray or in a deep tray or dish filled with rice or lentils.

Smoked Trout Rillettes Cones

MAKES 20

SERVE THIS VARIATION alongside the salmon cones, or on its own.

FOR THE CONES:

10 sheets brik dough (see headnote, page 93)
2 large egg whites, lightly beaten
¼ cup fine yellow cornmeal

FOR THE RILLETTES:

1 cup fish or vegetable stock
1 tablespoon unflavored gelatin
Juice of 1 lemon
Grated zest of 2 lemons
1 pound smoked trout, skin and bones removed
¼ teaspoon cayenne pepper
Fine sea salt
Freshly ground white pepper
Chopped dill

1. Preheat the oven to 400° F. Place a wire rack over a baking sheet. Spray 20 cone-shaped molds with cooking spray. With a small knife, trace an 8-inch circle on a sheet of brik dough (use an 8-inch round cake pan to trace around). Cut out the round, then cut it in half. Repeat with the remaining sheets of brik. Brush each half-round with some of the beaten egg white. Place the flat edge of the half-round vertically on a cone mold, about 1 inch down from its wider opening. The flat edge should fall straight down the mold, as a continuation of its pointed tip. Hold the flat edge securely to the mold, and roll the mold over the curved edge of the dough to create a cone. Repeat with the remaining brik and molds.

2. Roll the cones in the cornmeal (if the dough becomes dry, brush it again with some of the egg white to help the cornmeal stick). Lay the cones flat on the wire rack and bake for 8 to 10 minutes, or until they are golden brown. Remove from the oven and let cool. When cool, gently twist them off the molds. Make these up to 2 days ahead and keep them in a tightly sealed container.

3. Place the fish stock in a pot and sprinkle the gelatin over it. Let it sit for 4 to 5 minutes. Then bring to a simmer over medium-low heat to dissolve the gelatin. Remove the pot from the heat, add the lemon juice and half the lemon zest, and let it cool at room temperature just until the gelatin begins to thicken, about 15 minutes.

4. Mash the trout with a fork to break it into small pieces. Add the trout to the cooled gelatin. Season with the cayenne, salt, and white pepper. Then place it in a plastic pastry bag or a resealable plastic bag. Make the rillettes up to 1 day ahead and refrigerate.

5. Cut a ½-inch opening in the corner of the pastry bag, and pipe the rillettes into the cones. Garnish with the lemon zest and some chopped dill. Serve cold or at room temperature.

SEE THE PHOTOGRAPH ON PAGE 73

Fried Oysters with Lemon and Balsamic Vinegar

MAKES 20

OYSTERS ARE IDEAL FOR FRYING; their soft texture remains creamy on the inside while they turn crisp on the outside. Pair them with lemon, the perfect complement to any fried seafood, or balsamic vinegar, which adds both sweet and sour notes. ❈ Buy large oysters for this dish (the already shucked ones that come in plastic tubs are usually large enough). West Coast oysters, such as Kumamoto, are best for frying because they tend to be plumper. East Coast or Gulf oysters tend to be flatter and drier when fried. Whichever type you use, make sure that they are fresh.

1 quart canola oil, for frying
1 cup milk
1 cup all-purpose flour
Fine sea salt
Freshly ground white pepper
20 fresh oysters, shucked and drained of their liquor, or 20 bottled oysters, drained
4 lemons, thinly sliced (20 slices)
3 tablespoons balsamic vinegar

1. Fill a medium saucepan with the canola oil. Clip a deep-frying thermometer to the side of the pan, and heat the oil to 375° F.

2. Place the milk and flour in separate shallow containers. Season the flour with salt and pepper. Dip each oyster into the milk and then into the seasoned flour. Shake off any excess flour.

3. Fry a few oysters at a time in the oil until golden brown, 1 to 2 minutes. Do not crowd the pan, and maintain the oil at a steady 375° F. As they are done, remove the oysters to a plate lined with paper towels to drain. Sprinkle with salt.

4. Lightly crush the lemon slices with a fork. Sprinkle a few drops of balsamic vinegar on each slice.

5. Arrange the lemon slices on a large platter, and place 1 fried oyster on each slice. Serve immediately, so that the breading of the oyster absorbs the lemon and vinegar.

Hazelnut-Crusted Scallops with Pear Purée

MAKES 20

THERE'S NO NEED TO TOAST the hazelnuts in this recipe, because frying them brings out their flavor. Use large sea scallops rather than bay scallops, since they are bigger and more substantial.

1 cup sugar
1 Bartlett pear, peeled, cored, and diced
Fine sea salt
1 quart canola oil, for frying
10 sea scallops, cut in half
Freshly ground white pepper
½ cup all-purpose flour
2 large eggs, beaten
1 cup finely chopped hazelnuts

1. Place 2 cups water and the sugar in a medium pot over medium-high heat, and bring to a boil. Add the diced pear, reduce the heat to medium-low, and simmer until the fruit is very soft, about 12 minutes. Remove the pot from the heat and drain the liquid into a bowl. Reserve the pear cubes and the liquid separately, allowing them to cool to room temperature.

2. When they are cool, place the pear cubes in a blender. Add 1 to 2 tablespoons of the poaching liquid and a pinch of salt, and purée until smooth. You can make the purée up to 1 day ahead and store it, covered, in the refrigerator.

3. Fill a medium saucepan with the canola oil. Clip a deep-frying thermometer to the side of the pan, and heat the oil to 350° F.

4. Season the scallops with salt and pepper. Place the flour, eggs, and hazelnuts in separate shallow containers. Dip the scallops into the flour, then into the eggs, and finally in the hazelnuts, coating them well.

5. Fry the scallops, a few at a time, until golden brown, about 2 minutes. Do not crowd the pan, and maintain the oil at a steady 350° F. As they are done, remove the scallops to a plate lined with paper towels to drain. Sprinkle lightly with salt.

6. Place the pear purée in a plastic pastry bag or a resealable plastic bag, and cut a ⅛-inch opening in the tip or corner. Pipe a small amount of the pear purée on top of each scallop. Arrange on a platter, and serve warm.

Lobster Croquettes

MAKES 20

SHRIMP OR CRABMEAT can be substituted for the lobster here, if you like. I coat the croquettes in panko, Japanese breadcrumbs, rather than regular breadcrumbs, because they don't absorb as much oil and the food remains crisp. ❊ I cook a whole, live lobster for this dish, but you can also use frozen or precooked lobster meat.

One 1¼-pound lobster

FOR THE SAUCE:
2½ tablespoons unsalted butter
¼ cup all-purpose flour
1¾ cups whole milk

FOR THE FILLING:
Extra virgin olive oil
½ cup minced onion
6 large white mushrooms, cleaned and minced
Fine sea salt
Freshly ground white pepper

FOR THE BREADING:
2 quarts canola oil, for frying
1 cup all-purpose flour
4 large eggs, lightly beaten
2 cups panko

1. Bring a large pot of water to a boil over high heat. Place the lobster in the pot and cook for 8 minutes. Transfer the cooked lobster to a plate and let it rest until it is cool enough to be han-dled. Remove the meat from the tail and claws and chop it into small pieces. Place the meat in a bowl, cover, and refrigerate.

2. To make the sauce, melt the butter in a small saucepan over medium-low heat. Add the flour and stir for 6 to 8 minutes, or until the mixture turns a light brown. Whisk in the milk. Turn the heat up to high and bring to a boil. Remove from the heat and let cool.

3. Place enough olive oil in a sauté pan to coat the bottom, and heat it over medium heat. Cook the onion until soft and translucent, about 4 minutes. When the onion is almost cooked, add the mushrooms and cook for 3 minutes more, until the liquid released by the mushrooms evaporates and the pan is dry. Remove the pan from the heat and pour the mushroom mixture into a bowl. Let it cool for 10 minutes.

4. Remove the lobster meat from the refrigerator, and mix in the mushroom mixture. Add the sauce and mix gently to incorporate. Season with salt and pepper.

5. Line a baking sheet with plastic wrap. Spread the lobster mixture in an even layer on the pre-pared baking sheet. Place it in the freezer for 15 to 20 minutes (so that it solidifies and becomes more workable).

6. Remove the baking sheet from the freezer. Using your fingers or two spoons, take a small portion of the lobster mixture and roll it into a small ball, about the size of a large melon ball. Repeat with the remaining lobster.

7. Fill a medium saucepan with the canola oil. Clip a deep-frying thermometer to the side of the pan, and heat the oil to 375° F.

8. Place the flour, eggs, and panko in separate shallow containers. Roll the lobster balls in the flour, then in the eggs, and then in the bread-crumbs. Fry the balls, a few at a time, until golden brown, about 3 minutes. Do not crowd the pan, and maintain the oil at a steady 375° F. As they are done, remove the croquettes from the oil and place them on a plate lined with paper towels to drain. Sprinkle with salt.

9. Arrange on a platter, and serve warm.

SEE THE PHOTOGRAPH ON PAGE V

Fried Shrimp with Tamarind Dipping Sauce

MAKES 20

FRIED SHRIMP IS A CLASSIC PARTY food that is too often doughy and unsophisticated. This version is lighter and more unusual, thanks to the tangy flavors of the tamarind sauce and the use of panko. Tamarind is a sour pod that is used frequently in Asian and Latin American cuisines in paste form. Find the paste in the international section of supermarkets and in ethnic markets.

1 quart canola oil, for frying
½ cup all-purpose flour
3 large eggs, lightly beaten
2½ cups panko
20 medium shrimp, peeled and deveined
Fine sea salt
Freshly ground white pepper
2 tablespoons tamarind paste
1 tablespoon Dijon mustard
1½ cups extra virgin olive oil

1. Fill a medium saucepan with the canola oil. Clip a deep-frying thermometer to the side of the pan, and heat the oil to 375° F.

2. Place the flour, eggs, and panko in separate shallow containers. Season the shrimp with salt and pepper. Holding them by the tail, coat the shrimp with flour, then egg, and then bread-crumbs, always ensuring that the tails stay clean, which makes for a nicer presentation.

3. Fry the shrimp, a few at a time, until golden brown, about 4 minutes. Do not crowd the pan, and maintain the oil at a steady 375° F. As they are done, remove the shrimp from the oil and place them on a plate lined with paper towels to drain. Sprinkle lightly with salt.

4. With a whisk, mix the tamarind paste and mustard in a bowl. Slowly drizzle in the oil.

5. Arrange the shrimp on a platter. Place the sauce in a bowl on the platter, so the shrimp can be dipped in it. Serve warm.

Croques Salmon

MAKES 24

My FATHER FREQUENTLY MADE a traditional croque monsieur, with ham and cheese, for the staff of his pastry shop. While I love the classic version, I decided to give it a twist by using smoked salmon instead. The key is for the Gruyère to be very finely shredded, so chop it further even though the recipe calls for already shredded cheese. A full-size version of this croque also makes a quick dinner with a green salad on the side.

1½ cups shredded Gruyère
¼ cup heavy cream, whipped until thickened
Pinch of ground nutmeg
Fine sea salt
Freshly ground white pepper
6 slices white bread, crusts removed
2 tablespoons melted clarified butter (see page 6)
4 ounces smoked salmon, thinly sliced

1. Preheat the oven to 400° F.

2. Chop the shredded Gruyère very fine. With a spatula, gently fold the cheese into the thickened cream. Season the mixture with the nutmeg, salt, and pepper.

3. Brush 1 side of each slice of bread with the clarified butter. Spread the cheese mixture on the unbuttered side of each bread slice. Layer the salmon on top of the cheese mixture on 3 of the slices, and place the remaining slices on top, cheese side down.

4. Place each croque on a square of aluminum foil and wrap it tightly. Heat a dry skillet over medium heat, and cook the wrapped croque in it for 1 minute on each side. You want to get the foil hot so that it toasts the bread. Repeat with each package. Transfer the packages to a baking sheet, and put it in the oven. Bake for 15 minutes, turning them once halfway through.

5. Remove the packages from the oven and unwrap them. Both the top and bottom should be toasted and well browned.

6. Cut each croque in half lengthwise and widthwise, making 4 pieces. Then cut each piece on the diagonal to make 8 triangles. Arrange on a platter, and serve immediately.

Lobster Vol-au-Vents with American Sauce

MAKES 20

LOBSTER À L'AMÉRICAINE IS A CLASSIC French dish—usually much more complicated than the version here, which is made party-friendly by serving it in puff pastry shells so that the sauce does not spill everywhere. Make your own vol-au-vents or use store-bought mini puff pastry shells.

FOR THE LOBSTER:
1 carrot
1 celery stalk
½ onion, chopped
1 bay leaf
1 tablespoon black peppercorns
One 1¼-pound lobster

FOR THE SAUCE:
Olive oil
3 tablespoons sliced shallots
1 teaspoon chopped garlic
3 tablespoons tomato paste
¾ cup brandy
1½ cups fish or chicken stock
¾ cup dry white wine
1½ cups heavy cream
Fine sea salt
Freshly ground white pepper
1 tablespoon unsalted butter
1 tablespoon chopped parsley
20 Vol-au-Vents (page 11)
Chopped chives (optional)

1. Place 3 quarts water in a large pot. Add the carrot, celery, onion, bay leaf, and peppercorns, and bring to a boil over high heat. Stab the lobster at the cross mark behind its head to kill it. Remove the tail and claws from the lobster and place them in the pot. Cook in the boiling water for 3½ minutes. Remove the lobster from the broth and allow to cool.

2. Remove the lobster meat from the shells, reserving the shells. Scrape away the veins from the body. Dice the lobster meat into ¼-inch pieces.

3. Heat a ¼-inch-deep layer of olive oil in a large pot over medium-high heat. Add the lobster shells and cook, stirring often, until they are bright red, about 6 minutes. Add the shallots and garlic and cook for 2 minutes. Then add the tomato paste and cook for 1 minute. Add the brandy and let it reduce by half. Add the fish stock and white wine, and simmer for 15 minutes.

4. Remove the pot from the heat and strain the broth through a fine-mesh sieve into a bowl. Whisk in the cream and return the liquid to the pot. Simmer for 15 minutes over medium heat. Season with salt and pepper, and then whisk in the butter and parsley. Add the diced lobster meat, and stir until it is just warmed through.

5. Fill each of the vol-au-vents with some of the lobster and sauce. Decorate with chopped chives if desired. Arrange on a platter, and serve warm.

Scallop and Black Truffle Pizzas

MAKES 20

Scallops and truffles are an elegant combination, perfect for New Year's Eve or any other special occasion. The key is to slice the truffles and scallops thin enough so that they gently overlap each other on the dough round. For a less extravagant dish, top the scallops with a bit of store-bought truffle butter instead of using fresh truffles.

1 tablespoon unsalted butter

1 thyme sprig

1 rosemary sprig

1 garlic clove, crushed

1 leek, white part only, thinly sliced and thoroughly rinsed

Fine sea salt

Freshly ground white pepper

20 bay scallops

1 ounce black truffle

20 Parbaked Dough Rounds (page 9)

1 tablespoon black truffle oil

1 tablespoon fleur de sel

1. Preheat the oven to 400° F. Line a baking sheet with parchment paper.

2. Melt the butter in a saucepan over medium heat. Add the thyme, rosemary, garlic, and leek. Cook until the leek is very soft, 5 to 6 minutes. Season with salt and pepper. Remove from the heat, transfer to a bowl, and let cool completely.

3. Slice each scallop into very thin rounds, approximately 4 slices per scallop. Keep the slices of each scallop stacked together. Slice the truffle into very thin slices, using a truffle slicer or a sharp knife; you'll need about 60 slices.

4. Spread a thin layer of the cooked leek over 1 round of dough. Place a scallop slice on top of the leek, then a truffle slice, slightly overlapping. Continue overlapping alternating scallop and truffle slices until you have used all the slices of 1 scallop. Repeat with the remaining dough rounds, leek, scallops, and truffle.

5. Season the rounds with salt and pepper, and place them on the prepared baking sheet. Bake for 5 to 6 minutes, just long enough to finish baking the dough and quickly cook the scallops.

6. Remove from the oven. Drizzle a small amount of black truffle oil over each pizza, and top with a small pinch of fleur de sel. Arrange on a platter, and serve warm.

Leek and Oyster Tartlets

MAKES 24

SINCE THE TARTLET SHELLS can be made ahead of time, these are perfect if you have other time-consuming dishes to prepare. The soft, creamy leeks warm the oysters as they are spooned over them, and all the components of the bite come together in perfect harmony. Substitute precooked shrimp or crabmeat for the oysters if you prefer.

2 large leeks, white part only, cut lengthwise into thin 2-inch pieces and thoroughly rinsed
1 thyme sprig
1 garlic clove
3 tablespoons unsalted butter
½ cup dry white wine
½ cup white wine vinegar
2 tablespoons heavy cream
Fine sea salt

Freshly ground white pepper
24 oysters, shucked and drained of their liquor
24 Tart Shells (page 10)

1. Place the leeks, thyme, garlic, and 1 tablespoon of the butter in a saucepan over medium heat. Cook until the leeks are soft, about 4 minutes. Then add the wine and vinegar and raise the temperature to high. Cook until the liquid has almost completely evaporated. Then add the cream and reduce by half. Remove the pan from the heat and whisk in the remaining 2 tablespoons butter. Season with salt and pepper.

2. Place 1 oyster inside each tart shell, and spoon a small amount of the hot leeks over each. Arrange on a platter, and serve warm.

Seared Tuna with Tomato Confit

MAKES 20

Making a confit is a way of preserving food by cooking it for a long time in animal fat (as in duck confit), sugar, vinegar, or oil. Here oil-drizzled tomatoes are roasted for four hours to concentrate their flavor and bring out their inherent sweetness. The tomato confit can be made a day or two ahead and kept refrigerated. It is a perfect accompaniment to the rich tuna, while the crunchy phyllo adds texture.

FOR THE TOMATO CONFIT:

5 plum tomatoes, peeled, seeded (see page 6), and quartered

1 teaspoon sugar

Fine sea salt

Freshly ground white pepper

2 garlic cloves, very finely sliced lengthwise

2 thyme sprigs

2 rosemary sprigs

2 tablespoons extra virgin olive oil

FOR THE TUNA:

1 pound sushi-grade tuna

1 tablespoon cracked black peppercorns

Olive oil

3 sheets phyllo dough, thawed if frozen

¼ cup melted clarified butter (see page 6)

Fleur de sel

1. Preheat the oven to 200° F. Line a baking sheet with a Silpat.

2. Dry the tomatoes with paper towels and place them on the prepared baking sheet. Season with the sugar, salt, and pepper. Place 1 garlic slice on each piece of tomato. Arrange the thyme and rosemary sprigs over the tomatoes, and drizzle the olive oil on top. Bake for 2 hours. Turn the tomatoes over and bake for 2 more hours. This can be prepared a day or two in advance and kept, covered, in the refrigerator. Discard the garlic, thyme, and rosemary before putting the confit into the refrigerator.

3. Cut the tuna into 4 rectangles, each 1 inch wide, 3 inches long, and 1 inch thick. Roll each rectangle in the cracked peppercorns. Place enough olive oil in a sauté pan to coat the bottom, and heat it over medium-high heat. Place the tuna in the pan and cook it just long enough to sear the outside, about 20 seconds. Flip the tuna and sear for another 20 seconds. The middle of the tuna should be very rare.

4. Remove the tuna from the pan and place it on a flat surface. Arrange slices of tomato confit lengthwise on all sides of the tuna rectangles (you may need to use 2 pieces of tomato to cover 1 side of tuna).

5. Place 1 sheet of phyllo on a work surface and brush it with clarified butter. Keep the remaining phyllo covered with a slightly damp towel when not using it, to prevent it from drying

out. Place another sheet of phyllo on top of the first sheet and brush it with clarified butter. Place the third sheet on top, but do not brush it with butter. Cut the phyllo into strips 4 inches wide and 6 inches long.

6. Place the tuna with the tomato confit across the width of each phyllo strip. The dough will extend beyond the tuna by about ¼ inch at the sides. Roll the dough tightly around the tuna.

7. Place enough olive oil in a sauté pan to coat the bottom, and heat it over medium-high heat. Place the wrapped tuna in the pan and cook until the dough is golden brown, about 30 seconds on each side. Remove the tuna packets from the pan and place them on a cutting board. Trim the excess dough from the ends, and slice each packet on the diagonal into 5 pieces.

8. Sprinkle each piece with a small amount of fleur de sel. Arrange them on a platter, and serve warm.

Paella Cakes with Chorizo

MAKES 20

THESE SEAFOOD-RICE CAKES are flavored with traditional paella seasonings and then placed on a slice of Spanish chorizo. Prepare the paella the night before, and keep it covered and refrigerated until you are ready to cut it into rounds and sauté them. Purchase cleaned squids fresh or frozen at your fish market, or clean them yourself if you prefer.

8 littleneck clams, scrubbed

8 mussels, scrubbed and debearded

1¼ cups dry white wine

1 thyme sprig

1 garlic clove

2½ cups chicken stock

Pinch of saffron threads

Fine sea salt

Freshly ground white pepper

2 tablespoons olive oil, plus more to sauté the cakes

¼ cup minced onion

¼ cup finely diced red bell pepper, peeled (see page 6)

¾ cup Arborio rice

2 plum tomatoes, peeled (see page 6) and puréed

¼ cup finely diced zucchini

5 medium shrimp, peeled, deveined, and finely diced

3 squids, cleaned and finely diced

2 tablespoons grated Parmesan

2 tablespoons unsalted butter

1 large egg, lightly beaten

2 Spanish chorizo sausages, cut diagonally into twenty ½-inch-thick slices

1. Line a baking sheet with parchment paper.

2. Place the clams, mussels, ½ cup of the wine, thyme, and garlic in a medium pot over medium heat. Cover and steam until the shells open, 5 to 10 minutes. Drain, and discard the cooking liquid. Remove the clams and mussels from their shells and let them cool. Discard any that haven't opened. When they are cool, finely dice them. Reserve in a small bowl, covered.

3. Place the chicken stock and the saffron in a pot and bring to a boil over high heat. Season well with salt and pepper. Reduce the heat and keep the stock at a simmer; it will be used to make risotto.

4. Heat the 2 tablespoons olive oil in a pot over medium-high heat. Add the onion and cook until it is almost translucent, 3 to 5 minutes. Add the bell pepper and cook for 3 minutes. Add the rice and stir to coat it with the oil. Then add the remaining ¾ cup white wine. Cook, stirring constantly, until the liquid has almost completely evaporated. Stir in the puréed tomatoes. Then begin adding the simmering stock, about ¼ cup at a time, stirring continuously and making sure

the rice has absorbed the stock before adding the next ¼ cup. When the risotto is almost cooked, after 18 to 20 minutes, add the zucchini and diced shrimp and continue to cook just until the shrimp turns opaque, about 2 minutes.

5. Remove the pot from the heat and immediately stir in the squids. They will cook very quickly from the residual heat of the risotto, without having time to toughen up. Stir in the reserved clams and mussels, Parmesan, butter, and egg. Immediately transfer the risotto to the prepared baking sheet and spread it out evenly in a 1-inch-thick layer. Cover it with plastic wrap, smoothing it out with your hand to make sure the top is as even as possible, and refrigerate for up to 24 hours.

6. Preheat the oven to 325° F. Line a small baking sheet with a Silpat.

7. Place the chorizo slices in a single layer on the prepared baking sheet. Place another Silpat or a wire rack on top of the chorizo layer to keep it flat. Bake the chorizo until the slices are crispy but not too dark, about 15 minutes. Remove the baking sheet from the oven and place the chorizo slices on paper towels to absorb any excess oil.

8. Cut the chilled risotto into 20 (or more) small rounds with a ¾-inch cookie cutter. Place enough olive oil in a large sauté pan to cover the bottom, and heat it over medium-high heat. Sauté the cakes, in batches, on both sides until golden brown, about 4 minutes per side. Avoid crowding the pan. Add more olive oil between batches if necessary. As the cakes are done, place them on a plate lined with paper towels to drain.

9. Arrange the paella cakes on a platter, garnish each with a chorizo slice, and serve warm.

Phyllo Purses with Sea Scallops and Black Truffle Sauce

MAKES 20

THESE BITES, made with phyllo not crêpes, are similar to beggar's purses. ❋ Buy canned truffle juice and black truffle oil in gourmet stores.

FOR THE BLACK TRUFFLE SAUCE:

1 cup port wine
1 shallot, sliced
1 thyme sprig
½ cup truffle juice
1 cup veal stock
1 cup chicken stock
½ tablespoon black truffle oil
1 tablespoon unsalted butter

FOR THE PHYLLO PURSE:

6 sheets phyllo dough, thawed if frozen
1 cup melted clarified butter (see page 6)
20 sea scallops
Fine sea salt
Freshly ground white pepper
Olive oil

1. Preheat the oven to 375° F.

2. Place the port, shallot, and thyme in a small pot over medium-high heat and bring to a boil. Cook until the liquid has reduced by three-fourths. Add the truffle juice and reduce the liquid by half. Add the veal and chicken stocks and reduce until the liquid has a saucelike consistency and coats the back of a wooden spoon.

Strain the sauce through a fine-mesh sieve into another pan. Whisk in the truffle oil and butter. Set aside until ready to serve. You can make the sauce up to a day ahead and keep it covered in the refrigerator.

3. Place 1 sheet of phyllo on a work surface and brush it with clarified butter. Keep the remaining phyllo covered with a slightly damp towel when not using it, to prevent it from drying out. Place another sheet of phyllo on top of the first sheet and brush it with clarified butter. Repeat the process with the remaining sheets of phyllo. Do not butter the top of the last sheet. Cut out 20 phyllo rounds with a 4-inch cookie cutter.

4. Season the scallops with salt and pepper. Place 1 scallop in the center of each phyllo round. Gather the edges of the phyllo to the top, to make a small purse.

5. Place enough olive oil in a large ovenproof sauté pan to coat the bottom, and heat it over medium-high heat. Place the phyllo purses in the pan and brown their bottoms briefly, 1 to 2 minutes. Then place the pan in the oven and bake for 10 minutes to finish cooking the purses.

6. While the purses are in the oven, warm the truffle sauce over low heat. Arrange the purses on a platter and pour the truffle sauce in the center for dipping. Serve warm.

Kataifi-Wrapped Scallops with Orange-Mustard Sauce

MAKES 20

K*ATAIFI IS PHYLLO DOUGH* that has been very finely shredded.

FOR THE SAUCE:

Segments and juice of 4 oranges (see page 6)
One 1-inch piece fresh ginger, peeled and grated (about 1 tablespoon)
¼ cup sugar
1 tablespoon Dijon mustard
1 teaspoon sherry vinegar
Pinch of salt

FOR THE BATTER:

½ cup all-purpose flour
1 teaspoon cornstarch
¼ teaspoon baking powder
1 teaspoon salt
1 large egg yolk
1 drop Asian sesame oil

FOR THE SCALLOPS:

2 quarts canola oil, for frying
20 bay scallops
Fine sea salt
Freshly ground white pepper
1 package (1 pound) kataifi

1. Place the orange segments, juice, ginger, and sugar in a small saucepan and cook over medium-high heat until thick and slightly syrupy, about 15 minutes. Remove from heat and let it sit until warm.

2. Whisk in the mustard, sherry vinegar, and salt. Transfer the sauce to a bowl, cover, and refrigerate to cool completely, about 30 minutes. You can make this sauce up to a day ahead and keep it covered in the refrigerator.

3. In a bowl, mix the flour, cornstarch, baking powder, and salt. Whisk in ¾ cup water, the egg yolk, and the sesame oil, and mix until smooth.

4. Fill a large saucepan with the canola oil. Clip a deep-frying thermometer to the side of the pan, and heat the oil to 350° F.

5. Season a scallop with salt and pepper. Dip it into the batter and shake off any excess. Take a piece of kataifi dough, about 3 inches long and 1 inch wide, and gently pull the strands apart so they remain loosely connected. Place the scallop in the middle of the kataifi and wrap the dough loosely around the scallop. Repeat with the remaining scallops.

6. Fry the wrapped scallops in small batches, maintaining the oil at 350° F. As they are done, carefully remove the scallops to a plate lined with paper towels to drain. Sprinkle with salt.

7. Arrange the scallops on a serving tray or platter, top each one with a dollop of the orange-mustard sauce, and serve warm.

Basmati Cakes with Curried Crab

MAKES 20

THIS DISH IS EASY TO ASSEMBLE, and very quick if you prepare the basmati cakes the night before and the sauce a couple of hours ahead. The rice here is deliberately overcooked so it will hold together when you form the cakes.

1 tablespoon unsalted butter
2 tablespoons diced onion
1 cup basmati rice
2 cups chicken stock
1 bay leaf
1 large egg, beaten
2 tablespoons chopped parsley
2 tablespoons grated Parmesan
1 tablespoon crème fraîche or sour cream
1 teaspoon curry powder
4 ounces crabmeat, picked over for shells and cartilage
Olive oil
20 small dill sprigs

1. Line a baking sheet with parchment paper or a Silpat.

2. Heat the butter in a medium pot over low heat. Add the onion and cook until translucent, 3 to 5 minutes. Add the rice and stir until it is coated with the butter. Then add the chicken stock and bay leaf. Cover and simmer slowly for 20 minutes, until all the chicken stock is absorbed. The rice should be a bit overcooked and look almost like a paste.

3. Transfer the rice to a large bowl and let it sit until it is warm rather than hot. Then mix in the egg, parsley, and Parmesan.

4. Spread the rice mixture in an even layer, about ½ inch thick, on the prepared baking sheet. Refrigerate until it is really chilled, about 1 hour. Then cut out 20 rounds, using a 1½-inch cookie cutter. You can prepare the basmati cakes a day ahead, cover, and refrigerate.

5. In a bowl, whisk the crème fraîche with the curry powder. Gently stir in the crabmeat. This sauce can be made a couple of hours ahead, covered, and refrigerated.

6. Place enough olive oil in a sauté pan to thinly coat the bottom, and heat it over medium-high heat. Sauté the rice cakes, in batches, on both sides until golden brown, about 4 minutes per side. Do not crowd the pan. Add more olive oil if necessary.

7. Place the rice cakes on a platter. Top each cake with a dollop of curried crab, garnish with a sprig of dill, and serve immediately.

White Anchovy and Tomato Crostini

MAKES 20

THIS DISH FEATURES THE distinctive flavors of the South of France. You can find white anchovies marinated in white vinegar and tarragon in specialty stores, usually in plastic containers or flat tins. There's no need to rinse them before using them, unlike the anchovies that are packed in salt.

FOR THE TOMATOES:

Olive oil

1 shallot, minced

1 garlic clove, minced

4 beefsteak tomatoes, peeled, seeded (see page 6) and roughly chopped

1 oregano sprig

Fine sea salt

Freshly ground white pepper

FOR THE CROSTINI:

1 ficelle or other French bread, cut diagonally into 20 slices ⅛ inch thick and 1½ inches long

Olive oil

20 white anchovy fillets packed in vinegar

20 small oregano leaves

1. Place enough olive oil in a large sauté pan to coat the bottom, and heat it over medium-high heat. Add the shallot and garlic and cook until the shallot is translucent, about 4 minutes. Add the chopped tomatoes and the oregano. Bring to a simmer and cook slowly over low heat, stirring often, for approximately 45 minutes, or until the tomatoes thicken to a paste-like consistency. Remove the oregano, season with salt and pepper, and let cool.

2. Preheat the oven to 400° F.

3. Place the ficelle slices in a single layer on a baking sheet, and drizzle olive oil over them. Toast the slices for about 8 minutes, until they become crisp and a light golden brown. Remove from the oven and place the slices in a basket or on a plate until ready to use.

4. With a spoon, place a small amount of the tomato paste on a ficelle toast. Place an anchovy on top of the tomato paste, and garnish with an oregano leaf. Repeat with the remaining toasts, anchovies, and oregano. Arrange on a platter, and serve at room temperature.

SEE THE PHOTOGRAPH ON PAGE iii

MEAT

Every single one of these recipes is unique and innovative, from sophisticated and surprising versions of hamburgers and steak frites, to lighter fare like poached chicken, to an impressive foie gras terrine made in a microwave. If you serve only two meat dishes, vary the kind of meat they feature by including a poultry and a red meat preparation, for example. That's the secret to pleasing all your guests: If everyone finds something they like, they'll be happy.

Beef Carpaccio with Spinach and Anchovy Butter

MAKES 20

M Y FATHER MADE SIMILAR pinwheels when I was growing up, but he used white bread in them. I just use top-quality beef, spinach, and a flavored butter—a steakhouse menu. Keep the rolls on hand to serve if more guests arrive unexpectedly or if you run out of food—they can be sliced as needed almost directly from the freezer. Prepare them up to a week ahead and keep frozen.

3 anchovy fillets
4 tablespoons (½ stick) unsalted butter, softened
Fine sea salt
Freshly ground white pepper
5 ounces beef tenderloin, sliced ¼ inch thick
1 cup baby spinach leaves

1. Chop the anchovies very fine, until they form a paste. Place the anchovies in a bowl and add the softened butter. Stir until completely combined; then season with salt and pepper.

2. Place a 12 × 12-inch piece of plastic wrap on a flat surface. Lay the tenderloin on the plastic wrap, with the slices overlapping slightly, so that the meat completely covers the plastic wrap. Place another piece of plastic wrap on top of the tenderloin, and pound lightly with a mallet or a rolling pin until the meat is about ⅛ inch thick. Remove the top piece of plastic wrap and season the tenderloin with salt and pepper.

3. Spread the anchovy butter over the tenderloin in an even layer. Then arrange the spinach leaves over the anchovy butter.

4. Pull up one end of the plastic wrap and gently roll the edge of the tenderloin over on itself, as you would a sushi roll. Make sure that the spinach and butter are tightly rolled inside the meat, and take care not to roll the plastic wrap inside the tenderloin. Once it is tightly rolled and covered with the plastic wrap, place the beef in the freezer for 30 minutes, or up to a week. (If freezing for more than 30 minutes, take the roll out 10 to 15 minutes before cutting.)

5. Remove the roll from the freezer, remove the plastic wrap, and cut the roll into ¼-inch-thick slices. Arrange on a platter, and serve cold.

Vitello Tonnato

MAKES 20

Vitello Tonnato, sliced braised veal with a creamy tuna-anchovy sauce, is one of my favorite Italian dishes. I serve it in many ways, from sandwiches at the pâtisserie to canapés like these at parties. Top each bite with any type of greens you like.

Olive oil
8 ounces veal top round
Fine sea salt
Freshly ground white pepper
1 ficelle or other French bread, cut diagonally into 20 slices ¼ inch thick and 1½ inches long
2 tablespoons water-packed tuna, drained
1 tablespoon capers, drained and rinsed
2 tablespoons mayonnaise, preferably homemade
1 tablespoon lemon juice
1 tablespoon chopped parsley

FOR THE GARNISH:
4-ounce piece of Parmesan
1 cup micro greens, mesclun, parsley, or frisée

1. Preheat the oven to 350° F.

2. Place enough olive oil in an ovenproof sauté pan to coat the bottom, and heat it over high heat. Season the veal with salt and pepper. Sear the meat on all sides, 45 seconds to 1 minute per side. Transfer the pan to the oven and roast for 6 to 8 minutes, until the meat is medium-rare and registers 145° F on an instant-read thermometer. Remove the veal to a cutting board. Turn the oven up to 400° F. Let the meat cool, then thinly slice it. Cut the slices into small, very thin strips, and set them aside.

3. Place the bread slices in a single layer on a baking sheet, and drizzle with olive oil. Toast in the oven for 6 to 8 minutes, until golden brown.

4. Place the tuna, capers, mayonnaise, and lemon juice in a food processor. Process until the ingredients are incorporated. Place the mixture in a bowl, and stir in the veal strips and parsley.

5. With a vegetable peeler, peel off thin Parmesan shavings. Place ½ tablespoon of the veal-tuna mixture on each toast. Garnish the top with a Parmesan shaving and a small amount of micro greens. Arrange on a platter, cover, and chill for at least one hour or overnight.

6. Serve cold.

Duck Spring Rolls with Pickled Vegetables

MAKES 24

JUST TWO LEGS, not the entire duck, are used in this version of Peking duck. You can use any kind of duck, but Pekin is a fatty variety, with skin that gets crispier than other ducks' when cooked. Daikon, an Asian radish, can be found in the produce section of many supermarkets or in Asian groceries. Pickled ginger is what you are used to eating as an accompaniment to sushi: slices of ginger pickled in rice wine vinegar and/or sake, and tinted pink. Find it in the Asian section of your supermarket.

FOR THE DUCK AND SAUCE:

2 Pekin duck legs
Fine sea salt
Freshly ground white pepper
2 cups chicken stock
Three ¼-inch-thick slices peeled fresh ginger
1 scallion
2 tablespoons honey
½ tablespoon distilled white vinegar
½ tablespoon dry sherry
2 teaspoons cornstarch dissolved in
1½ tablespoons water

FOR THE SPRING ROLLS:

¾ cup rice vinegar
¼ cup sugar
1 carrot, cut into pieces 6 inches long and
⅛ inch thick
1 daikon, cut into pieces 6 inches long and
⅛ inch thick

12 sugar snap peas
4 scallions, about 6 inches long
4 rice paper sheets
12 pieces pickled ginger

1. Preheat the oven to 400° F. Set a wire rack on top of a roasting pan.

2. Rinse the duck legs under cold water and dry them thoroughly. Season the duck legs with salt and pepper, and arrange them on the wire rack. Place the baking sheet in the oven and roast for 30 to 40 minutes, until the duck is cooked to medium-rare and registers at 165° on an instant-read thermometer. Drain the fat and let the duck cool on the rack. When it is cool enough to handle, remove and discard the bones. Shred the meat into large pieces, and place them in a bowl. You can prepare the duck up to a day ahead and store it, covered, in the refrigerator.

3. Place the chicken stock, ginger, scallion, honey, vinegar, and sherry in a large pot and bring to a boil over high heat. Then reduce the heat to medium-low and simmer for 15 minutes. Stir in the dissolved cornstarch to thicken the liquid; cook until just thickened, about 1 to 2 minutes. Remove the pot from the heat, strain the sauce into a bowl, and let it cool slightly. Then cover and refrigerate until ready to serve. You can make the sauce up to a day ahead.

4. About 2 hours before serving, place the rice vinegar, sugar, and 1½ cups water in a pot and bring to a boil over high heat. Add the carrot and cook until tender-crisp, about 2 minutes. Remove pieces with a slotted spoon and spread them out on a flat surface, such as a baking sheet, to cool. Do not discard the liquid.

5. Repeat with the daikon, cooking it in the same liquid for 1 minute; then the snap peas, cooking them for 1 minute; and then the scallions, cooking them for 20 seconds. All of the vegetables should still be slightly crunchy. Spread them all out to cool.

6. Place ¼ cup hot water in a bowl and soak 1 sheet rice paper in it until it becomes soft and pliable. Depending on the water temperature, this will take between 30 seconds and 1 minute. Pat the rice paper dry with a kitchen towel and lay it on a damp towel.

7. Distribute one fourth of all the vegetables in a straight line near the bottom edge of the rice paper. Top with a few pieces of duck and pickled ginger. Slowly roll the rice paper over itself and the vegetables, making the roll as tight as possible. Set the roll on a baking sheet and cover it with a damp towel.

8. Repeat with the other 3 rice paper sheets and the remaining vegetables and duck. Keep the spring rolls covered with a damp towel to prevent them from drying out. Refrigerate, covered with a damp towel, until serving time.

9. Slice each spring roll into 6 pieces and arrange them on a platter. Spoon a dollop of sauce on each roll, and serve cold.

Poached Chicken with Green Apple and Curry

MAKES 20

OUR CATERING CLIENTS request this dish when they want maximum flavor and minimal calories. To cut calories even further, use low-fat coconut milk. Cook the chicken up to a day ahead. Let the chicken and the stock cool separately, and then store the chicken in the stock. The curry sauce can be prepared one day ahead and kept refrigerated.

FOR THE CURRY SAUCE:
Olive oil
1 shallot, sliced
1 garlic clove, chopped
½ teaspoon grated fresh ginger
½ teaspoon grated lemongrass
2 teaspoons curry powder
¼ cup brandy
1 plum tomato, peeled (see page 6) and chopped
½ Granny Smith apple, peeled and chopped (use the other half for the garnish)
2 tablespoons orange juice
2 cups chicken stock
1 bay leaf
½ cup heavy cream
¼ cup coconut milk
Fine sea salt
Freshly ground white pepper

FOR THE CHICKEN:
2 skinless, boneless chicken breast halves
Fine sea salt

Freshly ground white pepper
1 quart chicken stock

½ Granny Smith apple
1 tablespoon lemon juice

1. Cover the bottom of a saucepan with the olive oil and heat over medium heat. Add the shallot and garlic, and cook until the shallot is translucent, about 4 minutes. Do not let them brown. Add the ginger, lemongrass, and curry powder, and cook for 1 minute more. Add the brandy and reduce until the mixture is almost dry. Then add the tomato, chopped apple, and orange juice. Cook until the apple is soft and thoroughly cooked, about 5 minutes. Add the chicken stock and bay leaf, and bring to a simmer. Let the stock simmer for 20 minutes, or until it has reduced by half.

2. Meanwhile, place the cream and coconut milk in a separate pot over medium heat. Cook until the liquid has reduced by half, taking care not to let the cream boil over.

3. Once the contents of both pots have reduced, add the cream mixture to the stock mixture and simmer for 10 more minutes.

4. Put the sauce in a food mill set over a bowl, and pass everything through the mill. Then strain the liquid through a fine-mesh sieve into another bowl. The sauce should have a thick

consistency; if it appears thin, you can reduce it further to thicken it. Season the sauce with salt and pepper, let it cool to room temperature, and then place it in a plastic pastry bag or a reseal-able plastic bag. Refrigerate until ready to use.

5. Season the chicken breasts with salt and pepper, and place them in a pot. Add the chicken stock and bring to a simmer over medium heat. Cook slowly until the chicken is cooked, 8 minutes from the moment the stock simmers. Do not overcook, or the chicken will be dry and tough. Remove the chicken from the stock and let it cool to room temperature. Discard the stock.

6. Peel the apple half and cut it into small sticks, ¼ inch long and ⅟₁₆ inch thick. Place them in a small bowl and toss with the lemon juice to prevent them from turning brown.

7. When the chicken has cooled, cut it crosswise into slices ⅛ inch wide and 1½ inches long. Place an apple stick on each strip of chicken and roll up.

8. Place 1 chicken roll in each of 20 Chinese soupspoons. Cut a ½-inch opening in the tip or corner of the pastry bag, and pipe a small dollop of curry sauce on top of the chicken. Arrange the spoons on a platter, and serve at room temperature.

Foie Gras and Toro Granitas

MAKES 20

THIS UNIQUE IDEA comes from my friend Alex Atala, a chef in Brazil. He decided to put foie gras in a PacoJet, a professional type of ice cream maker, to see what would happen. The foie gras powder that came out was so good and so unexpected that I decided to try this by freezing the foie gras, which I pair here with sumptuous toro. Fatty and flavorful toro is the richest part of the tuna, found around its belly. The cucumber adds a crisp texture that complements these rich flavors. ❄ D'Artagnan sells foie gras in four-ounce packages or one-and-a-half-pound lobes. If you buy the larger size, use the rest in the other foie gras recipes, or freeze it for a month after tightly wrapping it.

8 ounces raw grade-A foie gras
Fine sea salt
Freshly ground white pepper
2 long seedless cucumbers, peeled
8 ounces sushi-grade toro (tuna belly), skin, bones, and sinews removed, very finely diced
2 tablespoons extra virgin olive oil
Fleur de sel

1. Season the foie gras generously with salt and pepper. Slice it very thin and place the slices on a baking sheet. Cover and freeze for 4 hours.

2. Cut the frozen foie gras slices into very small cubes, no larger than ⅛ inch, and return them to the freezer until ready to use.

3. Cut the cucumbers crosswise into 2-inch pieces. Scoop out the center of each piece, leaving a ⅛-inch-thick shell. Season the inside of the cucumber cups with salt, and turn them upside down on a rack to allow them to drain for about 30 minutes.

4. In a bowl, toss the tuna with the olive oil, and season with salt and pepper. Place a small amount inside each cucumber cup, filling the cup to the top. Spoon the frozen foie gras cubes on top of the tuna in a mound, and sprinkle with fleur de sel. Arrange on a platter, and serve cold.

Foie Gras Terrine in a Microwave Oven

MAKES ABOUT 1 POUND, OR ABOUT 8 SERVINGS

FOIE GRAS TERRINE cooked in a microwave? Yes, this method is foolproof and the foie gras is cooked in just 40 seconds! This works best when the foie gras is wrapped with a food vacuum sealer, but a resealable plastic bag can be used, too. ❀ To order foie gras, see page 167. Since you need only a pound here, use the rest for other cooked foie gras recipes.

1 pound raw grade-A foie gras
Pinch of sea salt
Pinch of freshly ground white pepper
2 tablespoons Sauternes

1. Let the foie gras sit at room temperature until it softens, about 2 hours.

2. Remove the veins from the foie gras by delicately scraping them with a small spoon. Place the foie gras on a plate. Mix the salt and pepper, and season the foie gras with the mix. Pour the Sauternes over the foie gras, cover it tightly with plastic wrap, and marinate overnight in the refrigerator.

3. Fill a large bowl with cold water and ice cubes to make an ice water bath. Place half the foie gras on a piece of plastic wrap and roll it tightly into a 1-inch-thick tube. Tie the ends of the plastic wrap into a tight knot. Place the tube inside a vacuum sealer bag and remove the air according to the manufacturer's instructions. Or place the foie gras tube in a resealable plastic bag and press out all the air with your hands; then seal the bag. Microwave for 40 seconds on high power. Then immediately submerge the bag in the ice water bath to chill it. Repeat with the other half of the foie gras.

4. Remove the tubes from the vacuum sealer or resealable bags, and refrigerate overnight.

5. Slice the foie gras terrine and serve it on brioche toasts with Tomato Chutney (page 152), or pipe it into tart shells, as in Foie Gras Mousse with Tomato-Strawberry Jam (page 141).

Foie Gras Mousse with Tomato-Strawberry Jam

MAKES 20

FOIE GRAS GOES WELL with sweet flavors, such as this tomato-strawberry jam. You can fill the tart shells up to 1 hour ahead and cover them with aluminum foil until you are ready to serve them. ❈ Serve this mousse on tart shells of all different shapes: barquette molds, as pictured, or square mini-muffin pans, for example. You could also serve the mousse on toasted bread: Toast slices of bread and cut out rounds with a 1½-inch cookie cutter. Pipe the foie gras on the toast rounds and top with a dollop of the jam.

FOR THE JAM:

Juice of 1 lemon

Juice of ½ orange

1 tablespoon cider vinegar

½ cup granulated sugar

2 tablespoons light brown sugar

4 ounces strawberries, hulled and quartered

10 ounces beefsteak tomatoes, peeled, seeded (see page 6), and chopped

1 cup Foie Gras Terrine (page 138) or purchased foie gras mousse, at room temperature

20 Tart Shells (page 10)

20 shelled unsalted pistachios (and as green as possible)

1. Place the lemon and orange juices, vinegar, granulated and brown sugars, and 3 tablespoons water in a small pot and bring to a boil over medium-high heat. Reduce the heat to low, and add the strawberries and tomatoes. Cook slowly until the mixture thickens to a jamlike consistency, about 20 minutes. Remove from the heat and let it cool slightly. Then cover and refrigerate.

2. Fill a plastic pastry bag or a resealable plastic bag with the foie gras. Cut a ½-inch opening in the tip or corner, and pipe some of the terrine into each tart shell. Spoon a small amount of the tomato-strawberry jam in the center of the mousse. Garnish with a pistachio. Arrange on a platter, and serve at room temperature.

Sirloin Crostini with Tapenade and Black Truffle Vinaigrette

MAKES 20

THIS, ONE OF THE FIRST canapés I developed, remains one of my favorites for this reason, but also because the earthy tones of the tapenade, Parmesan, and black truffle create an irresistible combination. ✱ If you don't want to use the truffle juice and oil, add a balsamic vinegar reduction to the vinaigrette: Place ½ cup balsamic vinegar in a small pot and cook over medium heat until it reduces to about 1 tablespoon. Whisk the reduction into the vinaigrette.

10 ounces boneless sirloin steak, trimmed, fat and sinews removed

Olive oil

1 baguette or ficelle, cut diagonally into 20 slices ¼ inch thick and 1½ inches long

FOR THE BLACK TRUFFLE VINAIGRETTE:

1 teaspoon minced shallot

1 tablespoon white wine vinegar

1 tablespoon black truffle juice

1 tablespoon black truffle oil

3 tablespoons extra virgin olive oil

Fine sea salt

Freshly ground white pepper

3-ounce piece of Parmesan

2 tablespoons tapenade, store-bought or homemade (see Note)

20 baby arugula leaves

1. Cut the sirloin into two pieces, each 1 inch thick and 2 inches long. Place enough olive oil in a large sauté pan to cover the bottom, and heat it over high heat. Sear the sirloin to medium-rare, 1½ minutes per side. Remove it to a plate, cover, and refrigerate. When the sirloin has cooled, cut it into thin 1-inch-long slices.

2. Preheat the oven to 400° F.

3. Place the bread slices in a single layer on a baking sheet and drizzle with olive oil. Toast in the oven for about 8 minutes, until golden brown.

4. In a small bowl, mix the shallot, vinegar, and truffle juice together. Then slowly whisk in the black truffle oil and olive oil to form an emulsion. Season the vinaigrette with salt and pepper.

5. Using a vegetable peeler, peel off thin pieces of Parmesan, to make 20 little shavings.

6. Spread a small amount of tapenade on each toast. Place 1 strip of sirloin over the tapenade, followed by 1 Parmesan shaving and 1 arugula leaf. Drizzle some vinaigrette on top. Arrange on a platter, and serve at room temperature.

NOTE: To make tapenade, place 1 cup pitted niçoise olives, 2 anchovy fillets, 1 tablespoon rinsed capers, and 2 tablespoons extra virgin olive oil in a food processor. Purée until smooth. Season with sea salt and white pepper.

Lamb Tenderloin with Endive, Roquefort, and Walnuts

MAKES 20

THE DIFFERENT TEXTURES here play with your taste buds—crisp endive, tender lamb, soft cheese, and crunchy nuts. Belgian endive leaves are natural receptacles for bite-size dishes. Create your own combinations to serve in them.

2 lamb tenderloins, trimmed, fat and sinews removed

Fine sea salt

Freshly ground white pepper

Olive oil

3 tablespoons walnut oil

1 tablespoon red wine vinegar

20 Belgian endive spears, each about 1½ inches long

Twenty ⅓-inch cubes of Roquefort (about ¼ pound)

20 walnut halves, toasted (see page 7)

1. Season the lamb tenderloins with salt and pepper.

2. Place enough olive oil in a sauté pan to coat the bottom, and heat it over high heat. Place 1 tenderloin in the pan and cook on all sides until it is medium-rare, about 1 minute per side. Remove the lamb to a cutting board and let it rest for about 5 minutes. Repeat with the remaining tenderloin.

3. While the lamb is resting, place the walnut oil and vinegar in a small bowl. Whisk to combine.

4. Slice the lamb into ¼-inch-thick pieces. Place 1 slice of lamb on top of each endive spear; then place 1 Roquefort cube on top of the lamb. Top the cheese with 1 walnut half. Drizzle a few drops of the vinaigrette on each slice of lamb. Arrange on a platter, and serve at room temperature.

Chicken "Jambonettes" with Soy-Honey Glaze

MAKES 20

THIS RECIPE IS A DRESSED-UP version of everyone's party favorite: chicken wings. *Jambonette*, or "little ham," is a classic French method for preparing chicken. The name refers to the shape of the chicken wing. These are easy to eat—the bone acts as a natural skewer. You can prepare the sauce a day ahead and keep it, covered, in the refrigerator. Reheat it over medium heat before serving.

FOR THE GLAZE:

⅓ cup honey
½ cup light soy sauce
Juice of 1 orange
1 garlic clove, minced
1 tablespoon Dijon mustard

FOR THE CHICKEN:

20 chicken wings
2 quarts canola oil, for frying
1 cup whole milk
1 cup all-purpose flour
Fine sea salt
Freshly ground white pepper

1. Place the honey, soy sauce, orange juice, and garlic in a small saucepan and bring to a boil over high heat. Then lower the heat to medium and simmer for 10 minutes, allowing the sauce to reduce slightly. Remove from the heat and let cool to room temperature. Whisk in the mustard, and reserve.

2. Break off the smaller of the two bones of each wing by twisting it. Discard it. Cut the skin at the skinnier end of the wing, and pull the meat down on the bone to create a hamlike shape.

3. Cut twenty 2-inch squares out of aluminum foil. Lightly spray each square with cooking spray, and wrap them tightly around the cleaned bone tip of each chicken wing.

4. Fill a medium saucepan with the canola oil. Clip a deep-frying thermometer to the side of the pan, and heat the oil to 350° F.

5. Place the milk and flour in separate shallow containers. Holding it by the foil end, dip each wing into the milk, then roll it in the flour. Fry the wings, a few at a time, until golden brown, 6 minutes. Do not crowd the pan, and maintain the oil at a steady 350° F. As they are cooked, place the wings on a plate lined with paper towels to drain. Sprinkle lightly with salt and pepper.

6. If it is much cooler than room temperature, reheat the sauce over medium heat for a couple of minutes. Remove the foil from the wings and dip the meat end only into the sauce, keeping the bone end clean to use as a handle. Arrange on a platter, and serve warm.

Duck and Almond Pastillas

MAKES 20

PASTILLA, OR BISTEEYA, is a savory Moroccan pie traditionally made with chicken. You can prepare these mini-pastillas, made with duck, a week ahead and freeze the filled, uncooked phyllo packets. Bring them to room temperature one hour before serving. Brush them with the egg wash, dust with confectioners' sugar, and bake just before you are ready to serve. Duck leg confit—meat that is cured and then slowly cooked in its fat and preserved in it—can be found in gourmet stores and many supermarkets. If you can't find it, ask your butcher to order it for you.

1 tablespoon unsalted butter
2 duck leg confits, meat removed from the bones and shredded
½ cup diced onion
1 teaspoon ground cinnamon
1 teaspoon saffron threads
1 tablespoon chopped parsley
1 large hard-cooked egg, chopped
¼ cup chopped toasted almonds (see page 7)
Fine sea salt
Freshly ground white pepper
3 sheets phyllo dough, thawed if frozen
4 tablespoons (½ stick) unsalted butter, melted
2 eggs, beaten
½ cup confectioners' sugar

1. Heat the 1 tablespoon butter in a saucepan over medium-high heat. Add the duck meat, onion, cinnamon, and saffron, and cook until the onion has softened, 3 to 4 minutes. Add the parsley, egg, and almonds. Season with salt and pepper. Remove from the heat.

2. Preheat the oven to 375° F. Line a baking sheet with parchment paper.

3. Place 1 sheet of phyllo dough on a work surface and brush it with melted butter (keep the remaining phyllo covered with a towel to prevent it from drying out). Cover it with a second sheet and brush with more butter. Cover that with the third sheet, but do not butter the top.

4. Cut the phyllo into strips ⅓ inch wide and 2½ inches long. You'll need about 100 strips. Lay 1 strip vertically, and place another strip horizontally on it, crossing at their centers. Arrange 3 more strips on top, crossing at an angle, to form a round shape.

5. Place the phyllo round on the prepared baking sheet, and spoon about 1 teaspoon of the duck filling onto the center. Brush with melted butter and fold all the strips toward the middle, to completely cover the filling. Repeat, to make 19 more packets. Brush the top of the packets with the beaten eggs and sprinkle with confectioners' sugar. Place the baking sheet in the oven and bake for 10 minutes, until the packets are golden brown.

6. Remove from the oven, arrange the pastillas on a platter, and serve warm.

Veal and Sweetbread Tartlets

MAKES 20

IN THIS RECIPE, veal round is combined with crispy sweetbreads and served in flaky tartlets. If you don't like sweetbreads, replace them with an equal amount of diced slab bacon, fried until very crisp. The flavor won't be quite the same, but it's a good variation.

Olive oil
8 ounces veal top round, cut into ¼-inch cubes
2 carrots, chopped
1 onion, sliced
2 garlic cloves
1½ cups veal stock
½ cup chicken stock
1 bouquet garni (1 bay leaf, 4 thyme sprigs, and ½ teaspoon black peppercorns, tied in a piece of cheesecloth)
Fine sea salt
8 ounces veal sweetbreads
½ cup all-purpose flour
1 tablespoon unsalted butter
Freshly ground white pepper
20 Tart Shells (page 10)
2 tablespoons chopped parsley

1. Place enough olive oil in a wide pot to cover the bottom, and heat it over high heat. Add the veal cubes and brown them evenly on all sides, stirring, for about 4 minutes. Add half of the carrots and onion and cook until the vegetables begin to brown and soften, 3 to 4 minutes. Then add the garlic and cook for 3 to 4 minutes more. Add the veal and chicken stocks and bring to a simmer. Then add the bouquet garni, cover, and simmer for 1½ hours.

2. Place the remaining carrots and onion in a small pot of water over medium heat. Bring to a simmer and season with salt.

3. Clean the sweetbreads by removing any connective tissue. Add them to the simmering water and poach (without ever boiling) for 6 to 8 minutes. Remove them from the liquid and let them cool slightly on a plate. (Discard the water and vegetables.) Cut the sweetbreads into ¼-inch pieces and coat them with the flour.

4. Place the butter in a cold sauté pan and heat it over medium-high heat. Do not let the butter brown. Add the sweetbreads and cook until they are golden brown, 4 to 5 minutes. Remove them to a plate lined with paper towels, season with salt and pepper, and let drain.

5. Using a slotted spoon, remove the garlic and vegetables from the pot containing the veal cubes, and discard them. Remove the meat to a plate. Reduce the liquid in the pot over high heat until it thickens slightly, about 3 to 5 minutes. Return the veal to the pot. Add the cooked sweetbreads to warm them up.

6. Fill each tart shell with a spoonful of meat, and sprinkle some parsley over it. Arrange on a platter, and serve warm.

Lamb and Tomato Chutney on Cumin Wafers

MAKES 20

T HIS IS ONE OF MY FAVORITE small bites, so full of warming flavors. We often serve it as an amuse-bouche at Payard, because the subtle spiciness of the dish opens the palate without overpowering any of the flavors to follow in the meal. Cumin wafers, made from lentil flour and spices, can be found at Middle Eastern and Indian markets or online (see Resources), most likely under the name *laxmi papad*. In a pinch, substitute small crackers. Elderberries are frequently used in Scandinavian cooking. You can find elderflower syrup in gourmet stores and in the food market section of the Swedish furniture retailer Ikea or online at germandeli.com.

FOR THE TOMATO CHUTNEY:

3 tablespoons olive oil

½ cup diced Spanish onion

8 beefsteak tomatoes, peeled, seeded (see page 6), and chopped

One 3-inch-long cinnamon stick, cut or snapped in half

One 2-inch-long piece lemongrass, crushed

One 1-inch piece fresh ginger, peeled and crushed

2 tablespoons rice vinegar

2 tablespoons elderflower syrup (optional)

Fine sea salt

Freshly ground white pepper

1 tablespoon chopped parsley

FOR THE WAFERS AND LAMB:

20 cumin wafers

1 star anise

1 tablespoon fennel seeds

1 tablespoon coriander seeds

1 tablespoon anise seeds

2 lamb tenderloins, trimmed, fat and sinews removed

Fine sea salt

Freshly ground white pepper

2 tablespoons olive oil

FOR THE GARNISH:

Fleur de sel

20 small mint or parsley leaves

1. Heat the olive oil in a pot over medium-high heat. Add the onion and cook until translucent, about 4 minutes. Add the chopped tomatoes, cinnamon stick, lemongrass, and ginger, and bring to a simmer. Reduce the heat to low and cook slowly, stirring often, for approximately 2 hours, or until the tomatoes thicken to a paste-like consistency. Mix in the rice vinegar, and the elderflower syrup if using, and season with salt and pepper. Remove from the heat and let cool. When the chutney has cooled, add the chopped parsley.

2. Preheat the oven to 350° F.

3. Place the cumin wafers in a single layer on a baking sheet, and toast them in the oven until they are crispy, about 5 minutes. They should brown slightly and begin to bubble. Remove from the oven and let cool on the baking sheet.

4. Place the star anise and the fennel, coriander, and anise seeds in a spice grinder, or a clean coffee grinder, and grind fine. Place the mixture on a plate.

5. Season the lamb tenderloins with salt and pepper; then roll them in the spice mixture. Heat the olive oil in a sauté pan over high heat.

Place 1 tenderloin in the pan and cook on all sides until it is medium rare, about 45 seconds per side. Remove it to a cutting board and let it rest for about 5 minutes. Repeat with the remaining tenderloin. Cut each tenderloin into ¼-inch-thick slices.

6. Place 1 teaspoon of the tomato chutney in the center of each cumin wafer, and arrange a slice of lamb tenderloin on top. Sprinkle a small pinch of fleur de sel over the lamb, and garnish with a mint leaf. Arrange on a platter, and serve warm.

SEE THE PHOTOGRAPH ON PAGE 125

Pork Burgers with Pickled Red Onions

MAKES 20

Lee Hefter, the chef at Spago Beverly Hills, inspired this dish. His pork burgers are so good that I just had to develop my own recipe. This unique variation on the ubiquitous burger makes it interesting enough to serve at more sophisticated gatherings. If you don't want to make your own bread, use mini pumpernickel loaves, or cut hot dog rolls into rounds as explained in the headnote on page 157.

FOR THE ONIONS:

1 cup red wine

½ cup port wine

¼ cup red wine vinegar

¼ cup sugar

1 red onion, sliced into ⅛-inch-thick rings

FOR THE BURGERS:

Olive oil

½ cup diced onion

12 ounces ground pork

2 garlic cloves, minced

Fine sea salt

Freshly ground white pepper

20 Black Bread Mini Burger Rolls (page 12)

1. Place the wine, port, vinegar, and sugar in a small pot, and bring to a boil over high heat. Add the onion rings, reduce the heat to medium-low, and simmer until they begin to soften, 3 to 4 minutes. Remove the pot from the heat and let the rings cool in the liquid. You can prepare the onion rings 1 day ahead; keep them refrigerated in their liquid.

2. Cover the bottom of a sauté pan with the oil and heat over medium-high heat. Add the diced onion and cook until translucent, about 4 minutes. Remove from the heat and let cool.

3. Mix the cooled onion with the ground pork and garlic. Season with salt and pepper. Shape the meat into twenty 2-inch patties. Place enough olive oil in a sauté pan to cover the bottom, and heat it over high heat. Place the burgers, a few at a time, in the pan and cook for about 1 minute per side, until done. As they are done, remove the burgers to a plate lined with paper towels to drain. Add more olive oil if your pan gets dry.

4. Place 1 burger on the bottom half of each bun. Top with 2 or 3 onion rings, then cover with the top half. Secure each burger with a skewer if desired. Arrange on a platter, and serve immediately.

Lamb Burgers with Harissa Dressing on Cumin Buns

MAKES 20

THIS DISH COMBINES THE traditional Mediterranean flavors of lamb, harissa, and cumin. Harissa is a hot chili paste; look for it in cans or tubes in the international section of your supermarket. The canned variety has more kick to it. Once it is opened, transfer the remaining paste to a plastic container, or it will oxidize. Harissa is very spicy; use it in moderation. ❄ If you don't want to make the buns, buy quality hot dog rolls and cut them into mini burger buns with a 1-inch cookie cutter. Cut the top and bottom separately and be very gentle so that you don't crush the bread. Brush them with a little bit of warmed olive oil seasoned with ground cumin.

FOR THE CUMIN BUNS:
2 teaspoons active dry yeast
3 tablespoons warm (110° to 115° F) water
2½ cups all-purpose flour
2 tablespoons sugar
1 teaspoon salt
3 teaspoons ground cumin
4 large eggs
8 tablespoons (1 stick) unsalted butter, softened

FOR THE HARISSA DRESSING:
½ cup whole-milk yogurt
½ teaspoon harissa

FOR THE BURGERS:
3 tablespoons olive oil
¼ cup chopped onion
10 ounces ground lamb
Fine sea salt
Freshly ground white pepper
Olive oil

1. Sprinkle the yeast over the warm water and let it sit for 10 minutes, until the yeast starts to foam. In the bowl of an electric mixer fitted with the dough hook, combine the flour, sugar, salt, 2 teaspoons of the cumin, and 3 of the eggs. Mix on low speed for about 2 minutes. Then add the yeast and beat on medium speed for 5 minutes, until a soft dough forms. Add the butter and continue to beat for 5 more minutes. The dough should be elastic and slightly sticky. Remove the dough from the bowl and allow it to rest on a lightly floured surface, covered with a damp towel, for 30 minutes.

2. Roll the dough out in all directions until it is ½ inch thick, and cut out 20 rounds with a 1-inch cookie cutter. Cover the cut dough rounds with a damp towel and let them rest for an additional 30 minutes.

3. Preheat the oven to 400° F. Line a baking sheet with parchment paper.

4. Beat the remaining 1 egg with 1 tablespoon water. Brush this egg wash over the rounds, and then sprinkle the remaining 1 teaspoon cumin over them. Bake for 15 to 20 minutes, until the rolls are brown and crusty.

5. Place the yogurt and harissa in a bowl, and whisk until well combined. Refrigerate until ready to serve. This can be done a couple of hours ahead.

6. Heat the oil in a small sauté pan over medium-high heat. Add the onion and cook until translucent, about 3 minutes. Remove from the heat and let cool.

7. Mix the ground lamb with the cooled onion, and season with salt and pepper. Shape the meat into 1-inch patties. Place enough olive oil in a sauté pan to cover the bottom, and heat it over high heat. Place the burgers, a few at a time, in the pan and cook to the desired doneness (about 30 seconds per side for rare, 45 seconds for medium, and 1 minute for well-done). As they are done, remove the burgers to a plate lined with paper towels to drain. Add olive oil if your pan gets dry.

8. Cut each cumin bun in half horizontally, and spread the harissa dressing on the bottom half. Place a cooked burger on top of the dressing, and cover with the top half. Secure with bamboo skewers if desired. Arrange on a platter, and serve immediately.

"Steak Frites" Sushi Roll

MAKES 24

ATING THIS CREATION OF catering chef Ken Tajima is like devouring a whole plate of *steak frites* in one mouthful, complete with the string beans on the side. You can prepare the meat a few hours ahead. If you do, warm it slightly before serving by reheating it on a baking sheet in a 350° F oven for about a minute.

One 14-ounce strip steak, about ¾ inch thick

FOR THE SAUCE:
Olive oil
2 shallots, sliced
3 tablespoons port wine
¼ cup red wine
2 cups chicken stock
1 cup veal stock
1 thyme sprig
1 tablespoon unsalted butter

FOR THE RICE:
Pinch of fine sea salt
1 cup sushi rice, rinsed
1 tablespoon sugar
¼ cup rice vinegar

FOR THE ROLL:
1 quart canola oil, for frying
1 russet potato, cut into matchstick pieces
Fine sea salt
2½ ounces haricots verts (very thin green beans)
Freshly ground white pepper

Olive oil
2 nori sheets, cut in half

1. Trim the steak on all sides to make a rectangle that is ¾ inch wide and 3½ inches long. Set the rectangle aside. Cut the trimmings into ½-inch pieces.

2. Place enough olive oil in a small pot to cover the bottom, and heat it over medium-high heat. Add the steak trimmings and cook, stirring periodically, until they brown and become deeply caramelized, about 5 minutes. Add half of the sliced shallots and continue cooking until the shallots soften, about 3 minutes. Add the port and red wine, and reduce until the pan is almost dry. Add the chicken and veal stocks and the thyme, and simmer for 45 minutes. Strain the liquid through a fine-mesh sieve into a bowl. Discard the solids. Return the liquid to the pot and reduce over high heat until the sauce coats the back of a wooden spoon.

3. Place the butter and the remaining shallots in a small pot over low heat. Cook very slowly until the shallots become very soft, about 3 minutes. Add the shallots to the finished sauce. Reserve the sauce, covered and refrigerated. You can make it up to a day ahead.

4. If you have a rice cooker, use it to cook the rice according to the manufacturer's instructions.

Otherwise, bring 1 cup water to a boil in a saucepan. Add the pinch of salt and the rice, and cook over low heat, covered, for 10 to 15 minutes, until all the liquid has been absorbed. Spread the cooked rice out in an even layer on a baking sheet, and let it cool for about 1 minute. Then dissolve the sugar in the rice vinegar, and drizzle this all over the rice. Stir gently with a wooden spoon, cover with a damp towel, and let cool.

5. Fill a medium saucepan with the canola oil. Clip a deep-frying thermometer to the side of the pan, and heat the oil to 300° F.

6. Fry the potato sticks, a few at a time, in the oil until they are crispy and brown, about 4 minutes. Do not crowd the pan, and maintain the oil at a steady 300° F. As they are done, remove the fries from the oil and place them on a plate lined with paper towels to drain. Sprinkle with salt.

7. Fill a bowl with very cold water and ice cubes to make an ice water bath. Bring a medium pot of water to a boil over high heat. Salt the water. Place the haricots verts in the pot and blanch for 1½ minutes. Using a slotted spoon, immediately remove the beans to the ice water bath. Let the beans cool for 5 to 10 minutes, then remove and pat dry.

8. Season the reserved steak with salt and pepper. Place enough olive oil in a sauté pan to coat the bottom, and heat it over high heat. Place the meat in the pan and cook on all sides until rare,

45 seconds per side. Remove the steak to a cutting board and let it sit while you roll the sushi.

9. Cover a bamboo sushi mat with plastic wrap. Place a half-sheet of nori on the mat. Cover three fourths of the nori with the sushi rice, and then flip the nori over so that the rice is on the outside of the roll. The section of nori not covered by rice should be closest to you. Place one fourth of the haricots verts on the bottom edge of the nori.

10. Pass a wet finger over the bottom edge of the nori. Pull up the bottom end of the bamboo mat and gently roll the edge of the nori over on itself, as you would a jelly roll. Make sure that the haricots verts are being tightly rolled inside the nori, and be careful not to roll the mat inside the sushi. Press the bamboo mat around the roll to form a square shape. Unroll the mat, and repeat with the remaining nori and haricots verts. You can do this a couple of hours ahead of time and keep the rolls refrigerated, covered with a slightly damp towel.

11. Cut the steak into twenty-four ¼-inch-wide slices.

12. Reheat the sauce over low heat. Roll each nori roll in the fried potatoes, and then cut them into 6 pieces each. Top each piece with a slice of steak. Spoon a little bit of the sauce over each roll. Arrange on a platter, and serve immediately.

Tartes Flambées

MAKES 20

TARTE FLAMBÉE IS THE ALSATIAN answer to pizza, featuring a flavorful combination of bacon, onions, and cream. It was one of my favorite tarts when I was growing up, even though I lived in the South of France. When I moved to New York, my Alsatian roommate and I used to throw parties where we served only tarte flambée and beer. For parties today, I make the tart in long strips and cut them into pieces. You can use slab instead of strip bacon for this recipe, and a small onion instead of spring onions. If you cannot find fromage blanc, place whole-milk Greek yogurt in a cheesecloth-lined strainer set over a bowl, and let it drain in the refrigerator overnight. The thicker, drier "yogurt cheese" will be perfect for cooking.

Olive oil

3 spring onions, bulb only, peeled and thinly sliced (see Note)

1 lean bacon strip, cut in half lengthwise and then into ½ × ⅛-inch strips

⅔ cup crème fraîche or sour cream

3 tablespoons fromage blanc

1 tablespoon coriander seeds, ground in a spice grinder, or ½ tablespoon ground coriander

1 teaspoon freshly ground nutmeg

1 small garlic clove, minced

Fine sea salt

Freshly ground white pepper

20 Parbaked Dough Rounds (page 9)

1. Preheat the oven to 400° F. Line a baking sheet with parchment paper.

2. Place enough olive oil in a large sauté pan to coat the bottom, and heat it over medium-high heat. Add the onions and cook until they begin to soften, about 2 minutes. Add 2 tablespoons water to prevent them from browning, and cook for another 8 to 10 minutes, until the onions are translucent. Remove them from the heat and immediately transfer them to a bowl so they stop cooking.

3. Place enough olive oil in a medium sauté pan to thinly coat the bottom, and heat it over medium-high heat. Add the bacon strips and cook until some of the fat melts away, about 3 minutes. You don't want the bacon to brown or become crispy. Remove it from the heat and transfer it to a bowl.

4. Combine the crème fraîche, fromage blanc, coriander, nutmeg, and garlic in a bowl. Season with salt and pepper.

5. Place the parbaked dough rounds on the prepared baking sheet. Spread some of the crème fraîche mixture over each round. Top with a spoonful of onions and a few strips of bacon. You can do this about 1 hour before serving and then bake the tarts as needed. Bake in the oven for 8 minutes, until warmed through. Arrange on a platter, and serve warm or at room temperature.

NOTE: Spring onions are wonderful long onions that look like fat scallions. They can be found in greenmarkets in the spring.

Mushrooms Stuffed with Braised Short Ribs

MAKES 20

INSTEAD OF STUFFING mushrooms with bread, I prefer to fill large caps with the meat of braised short ribs. Smash the garlic cloves to release their flavor, then remove them when you strain the liquid.

Olive oil
2 beef short ribs
1 carrot, chopped
1 small onion, chopped
1 celery stalk, chopped
3 garlic cloves, smashed with the back of a knife
½ cup red wine
1 quart veal stock
1 quart chicken stock
5 or 6 thyme sprigs
½ cup crème fraîche or sour cream
2 tablespoons bottled horseradish, drained
1 teaspoon lemon juice
Fine sea salt
Freshly ground white pepper
20 large white mushroom caps, cleaned

1. Preheat the oven to 325° F.

2. Place enough olive oil in a medium oven-proof pot to cover the bottom, and heat it over high heat. When the oil is hot, add the short ribs and sear on all sides, about 1 minute per side. Remove the ribs to a plate and set it aside.

3. Add the carrot, onion, celery, and garlic to the pot and cook over medium-high heat until the vegetables are browned and softened, about 4 minutes. Add the wine and reduce until the pot is almost dry. Return the short ribs to the pot and cover with the veal and chicken stocks. Bring to a boil. Add the thyme and lower the heat to a simmer. Cover the pot tightly or place a piece of parchment paper directly over the stock. Place the pot in the oven and cook for 3½ hours, or until the meat is very tender.

4. In a bowl, whisk together the crème fraîche, horseradish, and lemon juice. Season with salt and pepper. Place the mixture in a plastic pastry bag or a resealable plastic bag, and refrigerate until needed.

5. Remove the pot from the oven and raise the oven temperature to 400° F. Transfer the ribs to a plate. While they are still warm, shred the meat into small pieces with a fork.

6. Strain the ribs' cooking liquid through a fine-mesh sieve into another pot. Place the pot over high heat, and reduce the liquid to a sauce-like consistency. It should coat the back of a wooden spoon.

7. Cut a very thin slice off the top of each mushroom so it will stay flat and level when turned upside down. Fill the mushroom caps with the shredded short ribs.

8. Place enough olive oil in a large ovenproof sauté pan to cover the bottom, and heat it over medium-high heat. Place the mushrooms in the pan. You don't want to crowd the pan, so do this in two batches if necessary. Once the mushrooms begin to brown (after about 1 minute), transfer the pan to the oven to finish cooking. Roast for about 10 minutes.

9. Remove the mushrooms from the oven, and spoon a small amount of the sauce on top to keep them moist.

10. Cut a ½-inch opening in the tip or corner of the pastry bag, and pipe a small amount of the horseradish cream on top of each mushroom. Arrange on a platter, and serve warm.

RESOURCES

AMAZON
www.amazon.com/gourmet
www.amazon.com/kitchen
Chickpea flour, mini puff pastry
shells, cookie cutter sets, Silpats,
pans and molds, Chinese
soupspoons, tamarind paste

ASIAN FOOD GROCER
www.asianfoodgrocer.com
131 West Harris Avenue
San Francisco, CA 94080
T: 888-482-2742
F: 650-871-9154
E: info@asianfoodgrocer.com
Red and white (sweet) miso,
ponzu, panko, black sesame
seeds, nori, Chinese soupspoons

THE BAKER'S CATALOGUE
www.bakerscatalogue.com
P.O. Box 876
Norwich, VT 05035
T: 800-827-6836
F: 800-343-3002
E: bakers@kingarthurflour.com
Flours, cookie cutter sets, Silpats,
pans, molds

D'ARTAGNAN
www.dartagnan.com
280 Wilson Avenue
Newark, NJ 07105
T: 800-327-8246 x0

F: 973-465-1870
E: orders@dartagnan.com
Foie gras, truffle products, duck,
chorizo

FANTE'S KITCHEN WARES SHOP
www.fantes.com
1006 South 9th Street
Philadelphia, PA 19147-4798
T: 800-44-FANTE
F: 215-922-5723
E: mail@fantes.com
Molds, pans, baking supplies

GOURMET FOOD STORE
www.gourmetfoodstore.com
T: 877-591-8008
F: 954-241-6161
E: jonk@gourmetfoodstore.com
Caviars, foie gras, truffle
products, smoked fish

HOUSE OF SPICES (INDIA) INC.
www.hosindia.com
127-40 Willets Point Blvd.
Flushing, NY 11386-1506
E: info@hosindia.com
Cumin wafers (*laxmi papad*)

KALUSTYAN'S
www.kalustyans.com
123 Lexington Avenue
New York, NY 10016
T: 800-352-3451

F: 212-683-8458
E: sales@kalustyans.com
Tamarind, spices, poha, cumin
wafers (*laxmi papad*), kataifi
dough, sesame crackers, tamarind
paste, chickpea flour (*besan*)

**NEW YORK CAKE & BAKING
SUPPLY**
www.nycake.com
56 West 22nd Street
New York, NY 10010
T: 212-675-CAKE
F: 212-675-7099
Cookie cutter sets, Silpats, pans,
molds

PARTHENON FOODS
www.parthenonfoods.com
9131 West Cleveland Avenue
West Allis, WI 53227
T: 414-321-5522
E: sales@parthenonfoods.com
Phyllo dough, kataifi dough

UNITED GOURMETS, INC.
www.levillage.com
211 South Hill Drive
Brisbane, CA 94005-1255
T: 415-562-1138
F: 415-562-1137
E: orders@levillage.com
Brik dough (*feuilles de brick*)

INDEX

NOTE: Page numbers in italics refer to illustrations.